Settlement in the Forks of Mill Creek

A History of the Nelsonville Area

Austin County, Texas

by James V. Woodrick

ISBN-13: 978-1469956558
ISBN-10: 1469956551

Cover Image: Postcard from 1909, taken in front of Dr. John Kroulik's office on the main street of Nelsonville.

Table of Contents

February, 2005

A note from the author .....

My inspiration in researching the history of the Nelsonville area can be directly attributed to John T. Kroulik, PhD, son of Nelsonville physician John Kroulik. He willingly shared his lifelong passion in genealogy and in preserving the record of Texas settlement by Czech immigrants, as well as his personal childhood memories of the area and its people. His gentle nudging provided encouragement for me to proceed, and through him I was able to interview several individuals who provided invaluable information and other materials for this research effort. Included among these were Lydia Stalmach Maresh, Hettie (Mrs. Paul) Albert, Miss Rosalie Lesikar and Mrs. Gracie Jezek Hinze. My mother-in-law Sadie Kroulik Bravenec, and Edwin and Eslie Maresh Krause were always eager to share their knowledge of the area's history. John Dorroh provided information on his ancestor Flake family, as did Fred Burns on his family. O. B. Shelburne provided a wealth of information on the area and his ancestors, including a photo of the first dwelling built in the forks of Mill Creek and an 1895 newspaper article detailing the then-thirty year history of Nelsonville. Theda Conner provided information on her husband's great-great grandfather E. C. Williamson. Ray Stepan and Jerry Krampota provided information about their ancestors. Photos from the late 1800's to the 1920's of people and places in and around Nelsonville were obtained from a number of people whose parents or grandparents lived in the area.

James V. Woodrich

Settlement in the Forks of Mill Creek
A History of the Nelsonville Area
Austin County, Texas

Introduction

Nelsonville, Texas, is located in Austin County approximately eight miles west of the county seat of Bellville, on the oak-forested ridge between the east and west forks of Mill Creek. Communities nearby are Industry eight miles west, Oak Hill approximately two miles east and Bleiberville about four miles northwest of Nelsonville. Scranton Grove was an early community in the area on the East Fork of Mill Creek between Nelsonville and Bleiblerville. New Bremen and Travis were early communities nearby but across (outside) of the east and west forks of Mill Creek. The land area comprising the extended Nelsonville community begins at the juncture of the East and West Forks of Mill Creek and extends up the forks approximately half way to the town of Industry.

This history of the settlement of the land around Nelsonville focuses primarily on the lower portion of the land between the forks of Mill Creek, including portions of the Four League Grant to Stephen F. Austin and the adjacent George Grimes and Benjamin Eaton grants, comprising about 25 square miles. Further upstream within the forks of Mill Creek the settlers focused on Industry, Welcome and Wesley as the major community centers. Outside of the East Fork the focus was on the early community of Travis, later on the railroad-established town of Kenney. Outside of the West Fork the settlers in the New Bremen area looked to New Ulm and Cat Spring as the major community centers. Bellville was the dominant town to the east.

This account is primarily of the century from the first appearance of permanent settlers in 1838 to the peak of the strong Nelsonville community focus before World War II. The advent of the automobile, and in particular the opening of the paved highway in 1929 to the much larger town of Bellville, expanded the rural community's horizons. After 1930, the town of Nelsonville gradually declined as a social and commercial center in the region.

Most of the early settlers were farmers of British origin from the southern United States, and their slaves of African origin. After the close of the Civil War the economy of the region changed dramatically with the ending of the plantation system of agriculture. Many of the early white settlers left in the two decades after the Civil war but their former slaves, now freedmen, remained longer as farmers and laborers in the area. Continental European immigrants began to occupy the land after the Civil War, first primarily Germans but later almost exclusively Czechs. By the turn of the century, the population was predominately of Czech ancestry.

The 1880 Census for Precinct 7 of Austin County included the area in the lower forks of Mill Creek, and is summarized as follows:

- 1520 individuals in 285 family groupings
- Ethnicity of the "Heads of Household"

32%	Anglo, most from older southern United States
31%	Czech, most first generation immigrants
18%	African American
15%	German
4%	Other European countries and northern United States

The 1900 Census, as enumerated by J. A. Malechek between June 1 and June 20, 1900, in the "Nelsonville" precinct, is summarized as follows:

- 1396 individuals comprising 257 family groups
- Origin of the heads of household:

	% of total
Born in Bohemia	50
Born in Texas, father born Bohemia	10
Born in Germany	15
Born in Texas, father born Germany	5
Born in Texas, African ancestry	15
Born in southern United States, British ancestry	5

The Nelsonville area represented the largest concentration of Czech - speaking people in Austin County, and a spring-board for Czech migration to other parts of Texas. The first Czech immigrants to settle in Texas had arrived in Austin County in 1852, settling among the Germans in the New Ulm – Industry area. In the 1900 Census tabulation the name Bohemia is used to designate peoples from all Czech-speaking lands including Cechy (also commonly referred to as Bohemia), Moravia, Slovakia and Silesia. Austria is also commonly shown as the country of origin for Czech Texans in immigration and naturalization documents and the U. S. Census, as at that time the Czech lands were part of the Habsburg (Austrian) Empire. Austin and Fayette Counties were the primary areas of settlement of Czech immigrants before and immediately after the Civil War. Beginning around 1900, both new Czech immigrants and the children of the early settlers who needed new farms for the expanding number of families began to settle in other parts of Texas.

History of the Area Prior to Settlement

The land was originally claimed by Spain in the early 1500's, and remained largely unexplored by the Spanish through the early 1700's. Bands of Native Americans during this early period were the Mayeye and Yojuan (Tonkawans) living primarily to the north and west, Orcoquizas, Bidais and Hasiani tribes to the east/northeast, with Coco and Arkokisa (Karankawan) toward the coast. Tonkawans and Karankawans were primarily hunting and gathering societies living in much the same manner as they had for several thousand years. The Hasiani tribes lived in relatively permanent villages in the East Texas pine forests where they practiced agriculture, occasionally appearing in areas west of their primary territory. The Orcoquizas lived in relatively fixed villages growing some maise but living to a large extent on a fish diet supplemented by native fruits, nuts and game. At the time of Spanish contact, the Austin County area was between the major indigenous population centers, probably being crossed by traders and migrating groups from all directions. The two closest significant Indian villages mentioned in early Spanish records are near La Grange (a trade center frequented by several tribes from east and west Texas as well as two local tribes named Sana and Tohaha) and the Orcoquiza village of chief El Gordo ten miles east of the Brazos River on the headwaters of Cypress Creek.

The first European in the Mill Creek area could have been the Spaniard Cabeza de Vaca during his several year captivity with the Karankawa Indians in the Galveston area beginning in 1528. His memoirs indicate that he was involved in inland trade with other tribes during this period. The region between the Colorado and Brazos Rivers would have been a logical trade area from the coastal region, and Mill Creek is a major tributary of the Brazos.

In 1685, Rene Robert Cavelier, Sieur de la Salle, established a French colony on Garcitas Creek above Lavaca Bay in modern Victoria County. He made forays in 1686 and 1687 to the northeast in search of the Mississippi River in which he passed through the upper Mill Creek vicinity. Documentation of LaSalle's trips are not sufficiently detailed to precisely locate the routes that he traveled, but historians generally agree that these two trips went through or near the northern part of present-day Austin County. The Indian trail that became the Spanish La Bahia road seems a likely route.

Later, in the mid-1700's, the Spanish road between the La Bahia mission complex and Nacogdoches, the East Texas mission complex and Los Adaes (the mission/presidio near Natchitoches, Louisiana) passed through this area. The La Bahia presidio and mission were originally established in 1722 on Garcitas Creek in modern Victoria County, moved in 1726 to the Guadalupe River several miles north of Victoria and again moved to Goliad in 1749. Maps compiled by Steven F. Austin in 1829 and 1836 indicates the La Bahia road (also known as the "lower" Camino Real) went across the upper forks of Mill Creek near Shelby. Early land records clearly indicate that by 1840 the La Bahia road crossed the Colorado at La Grange and roughly followed the route of Hwy 237 through Round Top and Burton on to a crossing of the Brazos River at the town of Washington, just below the juncture of the Navasota River. The Spanish first used this Indian trading trail in expeditions to East Texas in 1690, 1692, 1693 and 1718. During most of the second half of the eighteenth century there was relatively frequent travel by the Spaniards between San Antonio, La Bahia and the East Texas Missions on the La Bahia road, and even more frequent use after the founding of Steven F. Austin's colony in the 1820's.

An Indian trading trail and Spanish road used at least occasionally from La Bahia to the Orcoquisac presidio and mission (occupied from 1756 to 1771) on the lower Trinity River near Wallisville passed through Austin County and probably near Bleiberville. This trail was first used by the Spanish in 1746 when Joaquin Orobio Bazterra, captain of the La Bahia presidio, was ordered to proceed to the mouth of the Trinity River to investigate rumors that the French had placed a settlement at that location near the villages of the Orcoquiza Indians. At this time there were three primary Orcoquisac villages; one at the junction of Spring Creek and the San Jacinto River near Kingwood, one about 20 miles up Spring Creek in the vicinity of Tomball, and one east of the Trinity River near Wallisville. Reaching the area after a long, circuitous journey (the Spaniards had not yet explored this area of Texas), Bazterra found no French settlers among the Orcoquiza but was told that the French had selected a site for settlement near the mouth of the San Jacinto. After traveling to this area and finding it unoccupied, Bazterra returned to La Bahia by a more direct route leading west to intersect the La Bahia road near Round Top. This route crossed the East Fork of Mill Creek from the direction of Bellville, probably passing near Bleiblerville, Welcome and Shelby. Spaniards continued to use this trail in the ensuing years after 1746 in their trips to trade with the lower Trinity River Indians, although during this period they also established the more direct route through Richmond and Houston today named "the Old Spanish Trail".

In 1767, the Marques de Rubi was directed by the Spanish Crown to inspect the presidios in Northern New Spain and make recommendations for changes in location reflecting the new political boundaries. Spain had acquired Louisiana from France in 1763, extending Spanish territory to the Mississippi River. Texas was no longer a "border state" and thus not as strategically important for protection of Spanish possessions. In October, 1767, Rubi left Orcoquisac for La Bahia. He followed Oriobo Bazterra's earlier route, crossing the Brazos River into Austin County on October 20, camping that night at a place they named "Vipernia", probably between Burleigh and Racoon Bend, logically at the location of the modern Hwy. 159 bridge over the Brazos. A showing the early trade and travel routes in this area indicates that Crump's Ferry operated at this location and modern roads through both Austin and Waller Counties merged at the river in this location prior to construction of the bridge around 1970. The Rubi expedition's engineer Nicholas de Lafora wrote in his diary on October 20 a warning of the dangers of the Aranama Indians, who would would slip unnoticed out of the heavy brush and weeds to steal the horses of careless travelers. Also on October 20 Rubi noted in his diary that the party killed both bears and deer. Marching west-northwest some 20 miles on October 21, the Rubi expedition camped at a place probably within the Mill Creek Forks they named "La Zorillia" – the skunk. The next day they continued their trip westward, intersecting the Camino Real near Round Top. The La Zorilla camp location was probably near Blieblerville, and would have been routinely used by later travelers on this road.

A group of 34 Acadians of French ancestry plus some 40 Germans traversed the Orcoquisac road in 1769. They had been on the English schooner ***Britain*** from Maryland bound for New Orleans where the Acadians planned to join relatives exiled from Nova

Scotia. The Germans were fleeing religious persecution in Maryland and sought to settle in Louisiana. Running low on supplies and at the mercy of an incompetent English crew, the ***Britain***'s captain refused to sail up a flooding Mississippi River and turned back into the Gulf of Mexico only to land instead at Matagorda Bay in Texas. They were initially detained some nine months by a Spanish garrison at the La Bahia presidio. In September, 1769, they were escorted from La Bahia to Orcoquisac, which they reached after 25 days, having traveled the usual route of that time through northern Austin County. After 5 days at the Orcoquisac presidio, they proceeded onward to be released at Natchitoches. A copper bar found by Gilbert Minton near Blieblerville on a rise about 700 feet above Spring Branch 0.8 miles southwest of FM 2502 (UTM coordinates 744600E, 3321800N) could well be an artifact lost by one of the travelers on the Orcoquisac road, perhaps at the "La Zorilla" campsite. The bar, 4 ¾" long, is engraved with the name "gerd davids" and an apparent date "1749". The French surname David was well established in Louisiana before 1800. Members of the David family are known to have been with the other French *Britain* families in Maryland and Louisiana.

Also interesting is the legend told by early Oak Hill settlers of an "Indian trading post" on the west fork of Mill Creek about two miles above the juncture, and the presence of metal artifacts of pre-1900 vintage (a key, square nails, a copper brooch) as well as arrow points and other Indian artifacts at this location.

The establishment of Austin's Colony by Stephen Fuller Austin in 1822 and 1823 marked the beginning of a rapid influx of emigrant peoples to this previously unsettled land. The earliest families who colonized the area received land grants from the Mexican government of a *league* and a *labor* as an inducement for their settling the area. The center of Steven Austin's colony was the town of San Felipe de Austin, on the west bank of the Brazos River just downstream from the confluence of Mill Creek with the river. The early settlers choose lands primarily on and between the Brazos and Colorado Rivers. Settlement on the major tributaries followed. Three of these early land grants included the land between the lower forks of Mill Creek. A league each was granted to Benjamin Eaton (May 16, 1827) and George Grimes (March 16, 1831). On January 15,1830, the Mexican state of Coahuila y Tejas granted five leagues and five labors of land to Empressairo Stephen F. Austin in payment for having colonized five hundred families in Texas, as agreed in a contract with the Mexican government dated June 4, 1825. One league consisted of 4,428 acres of prairie and timber land, while one labor was 177 acres suitable for cultivation, normally adjacent to a river or flowing creek. Austin selected four leagues of this total in the forks of Palmito Creek, as it was then known in Spanish, referring to the "little palms" which then and now grow profusely in the flood plains. The waterway became known in English as Mill Creek after a grist mill was built on the Cummins Hacienda near present Millheim.

In April, 1831, German immigrant Friedrich Ernst and his family along with Charles Fordtran arrived in Texas, explored the land in Austin's Colony and selected a West Mill Creek location because of its lush prairie, woods and ample water supply. Ernst acquired a league across the west fork of Mill Creek from the westernmost league in the S.F. Austin Four League grant and settled what later became the town of Industry. The Ernst homestead was quite isolated; during the early 1830s there were only two houses between Industry and San Felipe. Ernst was the first German to bring his family to Texas and came to be known as the "Father of German Immigration". He sent a letter back to a friend in Germany in 1832 which was published in a newspaper, widely read and is credited with sparking what soon became a flood of German immigrants to Texas. Among those who were attracted by this letter and came to settle near Ernst included the families named Bartels, Zimmershied, Juergens, Amsler, Wolters, Kleberg, von Roeder, Frels and Biegel. The families of Karl and Marcus Amsler, Ludwig von Roeder, and Robert and Louis Kleberg founded the town of Cat Spring in 1834. The son of Robert Kleberg and Louisa von Roeder Kleberg, also named Robert and born at Cat Spring, married Alice King, daughter of steamboat captain Richard King who founded the legendary King ranch in south Texas. Kleberg took over management of the ranch after the death of Captain King.

In 1831 or 1832, James Gotier established a road called the Gotier (Gocher's) Trace between San Felipe and Bastrop (then known as Mina). This road went through the nascent towns of Cat Spring and Industry and on toward La Grange, initially following the open country south of the timbered Mill Creek bottomland.

During the 1836 war in which Texas won independence from Mexico, one arm of the Mexican Army marched through Industry to San Felipe in pursuit of the retreating Texian Army. General Antonio Gaona arrived from Mexico in San Antonio on March 7, 1836, in time to participate in the Battle of the Alamo under the direction of Commander in Chief Antonio Lopez de Santa Anna. Following this Mexican victory, Santa Anna divided his army in pursuit of the retreating Texans under General Sam Houston. General Ganoa's battalion left San Antonio on March 24, 1836, for Nacogdoches with a brigade composed of the Morelos battalion, Guanajuato auxiliaries, one eight-caliber cannon, two four-caliber cannons with their respective equipment and twenty presidial soldiers, reaching the Colorado River crossing on the San Antonio - Nacogdoches Camino Real near Bastrop in a few days. On March 31, Ganoa ordered his engineers to build rafts to cross the river, and on April 9 he recieved word from Santa Anna to redirect and hasten his march to rejoin the rest of the Mexican Army on the lower Brazos River after taking the town of San Felipe. Ganoa crossed the Colorado on April 13, and marched down the river toward San Felipe. Some of the carts were lost in the crossing, which meant heavier loads on the remaining carts, hence shorter marches.

On the night of April 15, 1836, Ganoa's army camped near Mill Creek, having earlier that day torched the Ernst homestead at Industry. The precise route of Gaona's march is not known. Local legend has it that the army went from Industry to their April 15 camp near Nelsonville, then on April 16 crossing the west fork of Mill Creek at Sycamore Crossing. An alternate and more logical route would have Gaona staying on the then-established Gotier Trace, marching from Industry to the New Ulm area, then through Cat Spring and on to San Felipe. This route would have avoided the two Mill Creek crossings that the route through Nelsonville would have entailed. Accounts of early residents living in the Cat Spring and New Bremen area that tell of Mexican army destruction of their homes in 1836 lend support that Gaona went from Industry to San Felipe on the Gotier Trace. Regardless of the logic of the Gotier Trace route, many of the early Nelsonville and Blieblerville area residents shared the legend of "Santa Anna's" army passing through their area and perhaps burying some cannons or treasure at the Mill Creek crossings. Continuing from his Mill Creek campsite, on April 16 Ganoa encountered some dead Mexican soldiers hanging from trees and observed a large cloud of smoke from the retreating Texian's deliberate burning of San Felipe. Ganoa arrived at San Felipe on April 17.

Stephen F. Austin died on December 27, 1836, followed about six weeks later by the death of his namesake nephew and heir. In his will dated April 19, 1833, Austin directed the disposition of his estate, including the division of a large amount of property including the Four League grant in Mill Creek between his sister Emily M. Austin (Mrs. James) Perry and his nephew and namesake Stephen F. Austin, son of his brother James E.B. and wife Eliza Martha Westall Austin. A legal battle lasting several years ensued between Austin's sister Emily and Eliza Westall (with her new husband Wm. G. Hill) over ownership of the lands in the estate of Stephen Austin. The estate dispute was finally settled on September 1, 1846, with the four leagues in Mill Creek being deeded to Guy M. Bryan, son of Austin's sister Emily by her first husband. The delay caused by these legal proceedings resulted in the major portion of the land in the forks of Mill Creek being unavailable for settlement during the time that much of the Cat Spring, New Ulm, Industry and New Bremen area was settled. Even before he had clear title to the land, however, Guy Bryan began to subdivide the four leagues and sell portions to settlers. By the mid-1850s, most of the original four leagues granted to Austin was sold to settlers coming to Texas from the southern United States who then established homesteads and cleared the land for farming employing the typical slave-plantation economy of their origins.

The first Czech settler in the area was Rev. Joseph Ernst Bergmann, who left Europe in 1849 and arrived at Cat Spring in early 1850. He, like Ernst, wrote ardently enthusiastic letters about the Cat Spring area "home" to the Kolacny family and other acquaintances in Europe. Several of the letters were reproduced in Moravske Noviny, a Czech-language newspaper which was circulated in Moravia and Bohemia. He liked the climate - apparently he must have encountered some unusually mild summers. He was impressed with the abundance of available land with timber and water. He admired the local people, and especially appreciated the religious and political freedoms. By the end of 1848 many protestant Czechs felt that they had little chance of gaining relief from the authority of the Catholic church and the absolutism of Austria's repressive Hapsburg regime and were looking for places to emigrate. The encouraging letters about Texas from Bergman were welcome, and there was much enthusiasm about starting a new life in a new land. Meetings were held and plans were formulated for the transfer.

Much of this planning was done under the leadership of Josef Lidumil Lesikar, an advocate of Czech migration. The first group of 74 Czechs left for Texas in late 1851 on the ship ***Maria***, arriving at Galveston in early 1852 and finally reaching Cat Spring on April 5, 1852 after a devastating journey in which fewer than half of those who left Europe survived. About half of this group were members of the Silar (Schiller) family. Other Czechs on the ***Maria*** included those with surnames Coufal, Jezek, Lesikar, Mares (Maresh), Motl, Rosler, Rypl (Ripple), Silar (Shiller, Schiller), Szornovsky and Votava. Joseph Lidumil Lesikar and his family came with another smaller group of Czechs on the ship ***Suwa*** in 1853. Czech surnames in this second group include Busek, Cermak, Coufal, Janecek, Jares, Kroulik, Lesikar, Marek, Mares (Maresh), Pavlicek, Pechacek, Rypl, Silar, Slezak, Tauber and Zachar. Both of these first large groups of Czechs to come to Texas came from the Lanskroun and Litomysl regions of northeastern Bohemia – specifically villages named Horni Cermna, Nepomuky, Hermanice, Voderady and Dzbanov. Most initially settled among the Germans in the area around Industry, New Ulm, Frelsburg, Fayetville, Cat Spring and New Bremen. Members of these families and newer Czech immigrants after the Civil War, especially from the eastern Moravian region around Vsetin including villages named Hostalkova, Zadverice, Katerinice and Mikuluvka began moving to the Nelsonville area in the 1870's. By 1880 the area within 10 miles around Nelsonville represented the greatest concentration of Czech-speaking peoples in Texas.

Early Settlers (1830's to 1850's)

21 OCT 1837: Bryant **Daughtry** bought approximately 3000 acres on the outside of the West Fork of Mill Creek from Von Roeder and Amsler, the original settlers of Cat Spring. Although their land was not between the forks of Mill Creek, the Daughtry's were part of the area community. Son James Daughtry married Isabel Thompson and lived on land near Nelsonville inherited from her mother Jane, one of the early settlers. The Daughtry's were in Texas when James was born on July 18, 1823.

4 JUL 1838: The first settler who bought land in the area of the lower forks of Mill Creek was John Pamplin **Shelburne** (also spelled Shelborn). Shelburnes first came to Virginia from England (Wales) in the early 1600s. Unconfirmed family history says young Thomas Shelburne came to Jamestown in 1607. John P. and his brother Samuel Shelburne were born in Virginia about 1791 and 1793, respectively. Their family moved to Tennessee in 1805, staying until 1830 when they moved 100 miles down the Natchez Trace to newly opened lands in the northwest corner of Alabama. In 1837 they pulled up again and moved to Texas. With John was his wife Nancy, her mother Jane Dunkin and 11 sons and daughters ages 2 to 22. Others in the wagon train were the Houchin, Barnett, Minton and Terry families. In October 1837 they were in East Texas and applied for 640 acres of new land near Rusk. Later they cancelled this application and moved on to Austin County. John P. Shelburne purchased 921 acres (Lot 10 west of the S.F. Austin

Four League Grant) on July 4, 1838 between the West Fork and Blieblerville. Their homestead one mile southwest of Blieblerville was on a ridge separating Mill and Pecan Branches. In September 1842 John and his son-in-law Alfred Minton went to San Antonio to aid the Republic of Texas in repelling Mexican General Woll's forces from the city. Later, on December 25, 1844, he purchased the next tract (1198 acres, Lot 11 West) up the West Fork toward present-day Welcome. The Shelborn's bought more land in the 1850's and 1860's, and operated a major plantation - based farming operation. John Shelborn owned 14 slaves in 1850, and 24 in 1860. Samuel Allen Shelburne, John P.'s eldest son, married Adeline Bell of Bellville and raised 14 children in the area. William Lewis Shelburne, John P.'s second son, married Mary Catherine Terry from the nearby Terry plantation.

9 SEP 1839: Alfred **Minton** bought 435 acres on the West Fork of Mill Creek immediately downstream from the original J. P. Shelborn tract. Minton was born in South Carolina in 1803, and lived in Alabama before coming to Texas, where he married Jane K. Shelburne, eldest daughter of John P. and Nancy. Nancy America Minton, daughter of Alfred and Jane, married William Brookfield Fordtran, son of Industry co-founder Charles Fordtran and Almeida Brookfield. Another daughter, Virginia Ann, married Dr. Robert Thompson of Nelsonville.

1841: Alexander **Glenn** (1812 – 1894) came from Georgia to Austin County where he married Sarah Pamplin Shelburne (1819 – 1899) in December of 1841 and settled in the Mill Creek forks area. The Glenn's moved to Bellville in 1854, where they built one of the first homes in this new town. Glenn served as the Austin County surveyor from 1853 to 1860.

16 JUL 1844: John **Bell** purchased 125 acres of the Grimes League near the location of Nelsonville.

24 JAN 1845: Aaron M. **Logan** bought 125 acres on the West Fork just southeast of the location of Nelsonville. Logan was born January 1, 1800 in Tennessee and died September 13, 1881. He wife Elisabeth was born in 1825, in Alabama. In 1860, he owned three slaves.

9 NOV 1845: Mikajah **Terry** bought 545 acres on the West Fork. On February 7, 1847, Terry bought 574 acres adjacent to (downstream of) his original purchase; the northeast line of this tract borders the location of Nelsonville. On November 20, 1847, Terry bought additional land immediately south of the Nelsonville location. In 1850, Terry owned 8 slaves; ten in 1860. Terry and his wife Mary were born in South Carolina. A son William was born in Alabama in 1826, and two daughters Amanda and Martha were born in Mississippi in the middle 1830's. The Terry's arrived in Texas with the Shelburne family in 1837.

3 MAY 1847: Jasper **Daniel** bought 100 acres on the East Fork below Nelsonville. On November 30, 1852, he bought 640 acres on the East Fork below the Jane Thompson tract. On April 8, 1853 he bought 507 acres on the West Fork below the juncture of Long Branch. On March 3, 1859, he bought 1040 acres on the East Fork at it's juncture with the West Fork. During the mid-1850's, Daniel bought several smaller, adjacent tracts between the two forks of Mill Creek, and by the late 1850's his plantation included approximately three thousand acres in the lower forks. He owned 9 slaves in 1860. Around 1860 he began subdividing and selling his land, continuing this into the 1870's.

8 JAN 1848: James W. **Bethany** bought two tracts in the S.F. Austin Four League grant from Guy Bryan. The main tract of 562 acres bordered the West Fork and extended to the Grimes grant just west of the future site of Nelsonville. The second Bethany tract was 156 acres between the West Fork and Long Branch at their juncture. James W. Bethany was born in 1834 in Alabama. The Bethany family came to Texas in 1846 or 1847. Thomas Bethany, the father of James W. Bethany, was living in the area in 1850, at age 72, presumably with his son. He was born in South Carolina. Thomas Bethany owned 41 slaves in 1850, and , together with James, thirty in 1860.

21 DEC 1848: Elias **Elliot** bought 252 acres of the George Grimes League. On April 1, 1851, he bought 165 acres between the locations of Nelsonville and Oak Hill. On August 25, 1852, he bought 694 acres of the Four League grant for $694 from Guy Bryan. This tract was located on the West Fork at the juncture of Long Branch. Elias Elliott was born in 1828 in North Carolina and came to Texas sometime before the birth of a son in 1842. He owned 2 slaves in 1860. He and his wife Frances were born in North Carolina. Living with them in 1850, were Samuel Eliot (a schoolteacher, apparently not related) and son William, plus Joshua and David Ward.

4 DEC 1849: John **Ward** bought 418 acres from Guy Bryan on the East Fork at the lower edge of the Grimes League. He was born in North Carolina in 1820 and was in Texas in 1848 when his son Jasper was born. His wife Martha was from Tennessee. On December, 1850, Solomon Ward bought 150 acres north of Welcome. One of the Wards was an early surveyor in the area.

8 MAR 1850: William **Norcross** purchased 180 acres of the Four League grant from Guy Bryan for $180. Norcross was born in 1810 in New Jersey, coming to Texas sometime before the birth of a son George in 1846. He owned one slave in 1850. He owned land in the Grimes League in 1844, when John Bell purchased an adjacent 125 acres.

21 DEC 1850: John **Manley** bought 525 acres immediately southeast of Nelsonville. At the time of this purchase he was from Walker County, Texas. In 1860, Manley owned 7 slaves.

4 OCT 1851: Jane **Thompson** bought 646 acres on the East Fork between the locations of Oak Hill and Nelsonville. In 1865, the estate of Jane Thompson was divided among her children R. W. Thompson, Margaret Willis, Isabel Daughtry, W. A. Thompson, and George Foster (for his minor children by a Thompson, Charles and Fannie Foster).

24 SEP 1852: Ransom G. **Burns** bought 100 acres in the Kuykendall survey just south of the west fork of Mill Creek. He later bought 409 acres in Lot 4 in 1865, and a town lot in Nelsonville in 1867. Burns was born in either Virginia or North Carolina around 1800. He is listed as 48 years old in the 1850 Austin County census, and as 76 years old on his tombstone in 1874. He married Achsah Lee Bunn or Burn in 1834. She was born in 1813 in Goldsboro, North Carolina, daughter of Tobias Burn or Bunn and Anny Lee. Anny's grandfather's father was John Lee, Esquire, a large plantation owner southeast of Raleigh, North Carolina, in the early 1740's. Ransom and Achsah arrived in Texas November 18, 1841, first settling in the Brushy Creek community in northwest Walker County, where he applied for a land grant and was allowed 640 acres in Robertson or Fannin Counties. No record exists of his occupying this land. The Burns family moved to Austin County sometime after 1843. The Burns are listed in the 1850 Austin County census with 10 or 11 children. Thomas was born in North Carolina, Sarah, Narcissa and Frances in Alabama, Felix in Mississippi, and John, Nancy, Joanah (Joan D'Arch) and Tobias (Napoleon) in Texas. Mary Burns, age 24 and born in North Carolina was living with the family in 1850 with her 3 year old son John. Ransom Burns was a farmer, merchant and cotton broker. He may have had a store in Nelsonville, and son Napoleon is listed as a merchant in the 1880 census. Ransom died on March 31, 1874, and was buried in the Burns cemetery near his Oak Hill homestead. After his death, Achsah moved to Milam County to be with or near her daughters. Sons Thomas, Felix and John remained in the area. Felix and John joined the Confederate army (Company A, Elmore's 20th Regiment, in Galveston for duration of war). Felix married Helen Trott and lived on a farm on the Kenney-Travis road at Buffalo Creek; their youngest daughter Ollie taught at the Nelsonville school in 1911. Thomas and John moved to Bellville where John and wife Rosa ran a hotel.

28 JAN 1854: Thomas and Malinda Willingham **Flake** bought 203 acres and 25 acres on the East Fork near modern Oak Hill. Thomas was born in 1800 in Kershaw District, South Carolina. In 1840 and 1850 he was in Neshoba County, Mississippi, where he operated a plantation with five slaves. His grandfather Samuel Flake of Anson County, North Carolina, was one of the signers of the Mecklenburg Declaration of Independence. His father Thomas Flake lived in Lime County, Alabama and Kersaw District, South Carolina. The Flakes were listed in the 1860 census in "Forkston" as Thomas (age 60), Malinda (57, born in Georgia), Steuben D. (22, born in Alabama), Thomas M. (21, Mississippi), Elizabeth (19, Mississippi) and Lafayette (15, Mississippi). His occupation was "farmer", with real estate valued at $1550 and personal property of $9,800. On March 16, 1863, The elder Flakes deeded the following slaves to their sons Steuben and Lafayette: Nelson (32), Ferrel (24), Richard (21), Henry (21), Ann (5) and Jerry (3).

Steuben Flake was a partner with Issac Lewis and J. W. Bethany in the Nelsonville mercantile store. He married Mary Bethany, daughter of James W. Bethany; she died in 1865. He sold his property in Nelsonville on December 21, 1871, to Mathias Christopher and John Baletka, moving to Hayes County, Texas, where he died in 1879.

29 OCT 1856: Eldridge C. **Williamson** bought 87 acres from Elias Elliot near the location of Oak Hill. Williamson was born 14 Nov 1833 in Georgia, son of Eldredge Williamson and Nancy Clark Hart. He married Mary E. Johnson on 31 Oct 1854 in Washington County, Georgia. She was born about 1832 in South Carolina, daughter of Seaborn Johnson and Barbara McGraw White. They moved to Texas in 1854-55. Williamson's wife Mary died 8 June 1904 in Wesley, Washington County, Texas. E.C. died 16 July 1881 in Nelsonville. Their children were (1) Jasper N. Williamson, born 7 March 1855 in Nelsonville; married Annie S. Jones in Bellville, 3 January 1883. Later spouses were Carrie B. Power and Caroline (Lina) Wittenburg. Died 23 October 1924 in Thrifty, Brown County, Texas. (2) Nancy Catherine Williamson was born 15 December 1856 in Nelsonville; married Elbert T Creekmore in Bellville on 5 December 1877 and died in Bellville 17 July 1942. (3) Mary C. "Molly" Williamson was born January 1858 in Nelsonville; married C. Franklin Campbell in Austin County on 11 September 1879. (4) Georgiana Williamson was born 1860 in Nelsonville; married Tom A. Fincher in Texas on 10 October 1890; died in Burton, Washington County, on 4 April 1927. (5) Elizabeth F. Williamson was born October 1862 in Nelsonville; she married Louis F. Lee in Austin County on 8 November 1883. (6) Sarah Paulina Williamson was born August 1865 in Nelsonville; she married Marion Randolph White, Jr. in Austin County on 30 September 1887 and died in Texas 21 October 1940. (7) Eldridge C. Williamson, Jr. was born 24 January 1869 in Nelsonville and died 18 April 1889 in Jackson County, Texas.

The slave census of 1850 shows an E. C. Williamson owning one slave. Perhaps this slaveowner is Eldredge, father of E.C., who may have moved to Texas ahead of his family and was living in the area in 1850. His son Eldridge was 17 years old and still in Georgia in 1850; he married in Georgia in 1854 and did not move to Texas until around 1855.

During the Civil War

The Texas State Archives contain information on military troops in the Confederate Army throughout the state. The following records were found related to this part of Austin County:

The 23rd Brigade of the Texas Militia was raised in Austin and Washington County. Officers of the different "Beats" were elected on November 9, 1861. The following is a summary of the election returns from the archive documents. All of these Beats are part of the 2nd regiment.

Beat No. 8 Pecan Grove

Captain	J. N. Daniel	26 votes
	Wm. Thompson	6
1st Lieutenant	J. C. Brooks	27
	J. W. Bethany	1
2nd Lieutenant	J. W. Bethany	26
	J. C. Brooks	1
	John Manley	1
?? 2nd Lieutenant	Thomas Bradbury	26

Signed by J. N. Daniel, Presiding officer, Jno Manley, H. J. T. Terry, L A. Cumings, J. W. Bethany

Beat No. 7, Catsprings

Captain	E. L. Theumann	32 votes
	H. Welhausen	1
1st Lieutenant	A. Bock	17
	R. Goebel	11
	C. Meister	2
	Kleifer	3
2nd Lieutenant	Chas. Meister	15
	A. Bock	14
	C. Palm	1
	R. Goebel	2
	Kleifer	1
?? & 2nd Lieutenant	Kliefer	18
	Meister	12
	C. Palm	2
	Bock	`

Signed by M. Hartman, Presiding Officer, B. Legert, H. Welhausen, E. G. Maetze, C. Palm.

Beat No. 9, Precinct of New Ulm

Captian	Fred. Mittanck		65 votes
	Adam Wangsmann		28
1st Lieutenant	Louis Meier		66
	T. Dent	27	
	F. Wolters		1
2nd Lieutenant	T. Horning		66
	W. Fahrenhotz		28
?? 2nd Lieutenant	Gottleib Schroeder		66
	M. Meissner		28

Signed by Robert Berner, Presiding Officer, Max Meissner, H. Hinkle, Hermann Lechant, John Brod.

Beat No. 10 - Buckhorn

Captain	S. Graff	20
	Wm. Jackson	1
	Shoprer	4
1st Lieutenant	Wm. Pearson	16
	G. Byers	9
2nd Lieutenant	W. Cochran	21
	T. Wiggens	2
?? & 2nd Lieutenant	L. D. Sloan	22
	W. Cochran	1
	G. Byers	1

Signed by W. Cochran, Presiding officer, A. Cocke, M. L. Lerek

Beat No. 3 - Shelby's – no returns. Industry:

Captain	Robert Voight	29
	S. E. Daniels	2
	C. Leptner	1
1st Lieutenant	E. Shearer	27
	C. Kubitz	2
	W. Norcross	1
	C. Leptner	1
	C. Dettmar	1
2nd Lieutenant	C. Kubitz	16
	A. Hermenberg	11
	C. Leptner	2
	S. E. Daniels	1
	F. Fischafs	1
	C. Koch	1
?? & 2nd Lieutenant	Chas. Leptner	27
	S. E. Daniels	2
	C. Kubitz	1
	F. Knolle	1
	F. Tegge	1

Signed Robert Voight, Presiding Officer, James Daughtry, E. Scherer, S. E. Daniel, Chas. Dettmar.

Beat No. 5 - Bellville

Captian	F. Hariegel	38
	H. Miller	9
	P. Palm	1
1st Lieutenant	A. Schenk	24
	H. Viereck	7

	B. T. Harris	2
	T. E. Koch	1
	H. Miller	1
	J. Harloff	1
2nd Lieutenant	H. Viereck	34
	W. Matthews	1
	H. Mahnke	6
	A. Schenk	3
	G. Koch	1
?? & 2nd Lieutenant	J. Harloff	29
	H. Mahnke	4
	B. Granville	1
	H. Viereck	3

Signed by B. F. Elliott, Presiding Officer, W.L.M. Lyons, T.E. Dickehut, B. Granville, B. Fischer

Beat No. 2 - Travis (30 votes) and Sempronius (11 votes)

Captain	H. E. L??tzer	28
	I. F. Edwards, Jr.	6
	Jno Campbell	5
	E. Clearland	2
1st Lieutenant	W. T. Campbell	23
	P. C. Hickman	17
	Sam. Miller	1
2nd Lieutenant	John R. Campbell	23
	E. P. Scabs	11
	Sam Miller	5
	P. E. Hickman	2
?? & 2nd Lieutenant	L. Sam	20
	G. C. Thornton	11
	P. E. Hickman	4
	S. W. Miller	3
	J. R. Campbell	1
	Thos. E. Woods	1

Signed for Travis: E. Cevavlaus, Presiding Officer, Geo. W. Lott, D. L. Purcell, N. H. Murray. Signed for Sempronius: P. E. Hickman, Presiding Officer, E. P. Scabs, N. H. Murray, T. W. Ruke.

Several Czech immigrants living in the extended area around Industry also served in the Civil War, although not by their own volition. They opposed slavery but were forcibly "conscripted" by Confederate army organizers. One such conscript, Jan Kroulik, arrived in 1853 from Bohemia and lived on a farm west of Industry. He writes of his Civil War experiences as follows: "It was in the spring of 1862 when it was announced that all men between the ages of 18 and 35 will be taken into the army. We Czechoslovaks, who were settled here, felt on the side of the North and did not believe that we would be forced to serve in the Southern army. Soon after that I saw a group of riders coming to my house. I quickly hid myself, but they left orders for me to report to the army the next day. I was hiding in the forest for seven days because I did not wish to bear arms against the Union. Since they continued to come to my house and threatened my mother, I decided to yield and to join the army. I was added to Texas Wolf's (Waul's) Legion, Regiment Section D. In this section there were 15 Czechs out of a total of 23. We started out on that long and dangerous march. The first night we bedded down but did not sleep because four of our men were thinking of escaping and were waiting for a convenient time. Those four were Karl and Vincenc Lesikar (sons of the J.L. Lesikar) and two of the Votypka brothers. They succeeded in escaping during the night and even though a group of riders was sent out after them, the Czech escapees seemed to have disappeared from the earth; they were not found."

Waul's Texas Legion fell into captivity at the surrender of Vicksburg. John Kroulik personally asked General Grant to permit him to join the North because he knew that as soon as the Southern prisoners were released they would be forced back into service against the Union. Grant refused because he felt that it would represent the breaking of an agreement (Jan's Confederate army enlistment oath). There was nothing for Kroulik to do but to escape the army and hide in Texas until he would no longer be hunted. He walked from Vicksburg with Vaclav Votypka and John Mikeska and they reached home safely. But now they had to stay in hiding for the Confederacy desperately needed an army and whoever was found was removed from home without any mercy and forced into the service.

"As soon as we came home everyone was telling us that we will be forced to return to the army, and it was true. Anyone who did not volunteer was sent after. In the spring of 1864 the rebels acted without any consideration; they sent soldiers into the homes and they remained there until the deserters returned. Needless to say, the rough soldiers mistreated all members of the family to help the return of the deserters. Property was needlessly destroyed. One day several of them dashed to my brother-in-law, Vaclav Janecek and ordered him to tell where the deserters were hidden. At that time I was hidden under the floor in the stable. I could hear them as they talked and were walking around taking care of their horses. I had to stay there until the night came and I was breathing quietly expecting to be discovered at any moment. It did not happen and at night when they went into the house to eat, I slowly came out and after carefully covering my hiding place, I ran into the woods nearby. As several days passed by and the soldiers did not leave, my brother-in-law went to Houston to the headquarters and complained how his family suffered with the soldiers and before he returned they were gone. Now things got a little better. When we would hear that the enforcers were coming we fled into the woods and hid in the thickets where we waited until they left. There were people here who gave reports to the soldiers as soon as we returned home but others again gave us warnings, when to leave. During the night of July 13 to 14 Thomas Votypka and I dared to enter the home of my partner and, as everything was quiet, we spent the night. Early in the morning as we planned to leave after breakfast, I looked out of the window and to my surprise I saw the rebels coming over the fence. "The catchers are here!" I called and we ran into the fields as fast as our feet could carry us. The rebels fired several shots after us which only speeded us up a little more. They caught Votypka and I entered a corn field through which I reached the woods nearby thinking that would be my safety.

As soon as I crossed one little thicket I saw a soldier standing before me. He had been left behind guarding the horses. At that moment I did not know what to do. I saw that the rebel had a gun, but I still would have tried to run if I would not have seen the three large bloodhounds which he had with him. At that moment other soldiers came to get the dogs to trace someone who had escaped into the woods. As I happened to be the one who escaped, there was no need to release the dogs. Thomas Votypka had been wounded in the shoulder. We were tied together and led to the camp. From the camp we were taken to Galveston to be brought for an army trial. Votypka got sick with yellow fever and was taken to the hospital where he died later. I was told everywhere that I was going to be shot to death, which according to existing conditions among the rebels was quite ordinary. There was a German soldier here who was also condemned to die. Before the time of our trial, an epidemic of yellow fever broke out in Galveston and we were taken to a camp about two miles from Houston. From there John Votypka was able to escape. The epidemic spread to the camp also and we had to be deported to Millican, northeast of Houston, where we were put into a warehouse. Guards were placed all around so there was no thought of escape now, nevertheless, I waited for the first frost when I would attempt to escape. With the help of a few Germans who had the same idea, we cut an opening through the floor and on November 27 I lowered myself down first and before I knew it I was outside. I waited until the guards scattered and then started crawling on the ground, holding my blanket in my teeth and expecting a bullet to whiz by at any minute. It did not happen and I found myself free and did not know which way to turn. I did not dare to walk along the road for anyone going anywhere had to have a pass. On the other hand I had the deep river Brazos and at each crossing there was a guard. I walked around all night and in the morning I hid in a thicket and decided to wait for the night. I was surprised however when I heard the noise of a train at Millican. I must have been walking in a circle around the town, while I thought I was walking away from it. Several hunters went around with dogs and even though they came close to my hiding place I was unnoticed and thus saved. After a long walk I reached the river bank. I swam the river and gladly started another walk. I had suffered a lot and was afraid. One morning during a heavy fog I heard a horn blowing; again I knew I was near the rebel camp and so as not to fall right into their hands I came to a high cedar tree in which I spent the whole day. Finally after nine days and nights I found myself among my own again. In those nine days I had eaten only two ears of corn which I had found in the field, but I suffered most with thirst. Once I did not find a drop of water for three days. I felt the results for a long period of time. As soon as I was thirsty and did not get a drink right away my whole body started shaking and I had to rest immediately. From that day I kept on hiding every day until the war was over."

Founding of Nelsonville in 1865

The post office location for the 1860 census in the area that later became Nelsonville was called Forkston, in the Pecan Grove Precinct, probably referring to a "town in the forks" of the creek, perhaps by Pecan Creek near the John P. Shelburne homestead. This name did not stick, however, and could have referred to what later became Nelsonville, Blieblerville, Oak Hill, Scranton Grove, or simply the grouping of settlers in this area who had yet to establish a central community focus. David D. Nelson constructed the first building in 1865 in the nascent community that later took his name. Nelson was born in Georgia in 1824, and his wife Sarah was born in Alabama in 1834; their daughter Sarah was born in Texas in 1859. Early Texas records mention a resident of Austin County in 1826 named James Nelson who was a widower, farmer and stockraiser between 25 and 40 years old who had one son and two daughters between the ages of one and seven. Perhaps this was David Nelson's father. The Nelson building built in 1865 had two rooms, one in which the family occupied and the other used as a mercantile store.

Issac Lewis built the first store in Nelsonville in 1866, and was the first postmaster in 1872. Lewis was born in Poland and immigrated in 1852. Fritz Lindemann and a Mr. Faucett followed with other businesses; Lewis later moved to Bellville. The town of Nelsonville was platted and the Nelson's began selling lots in 1867 (see detailed lot sales records in the appendix). In the 1860s and 1870s a large number of German and Czech immigrants moved into the area, buying land when the families from the older southern states gradually moved away as the economy changed with the freeing of slaves after the Civil War. As Nelsonville grew into a community, there was discussion of moving the county seat there from Bellville. Spurred by the removal of the portion of Austin County east of the Brazos to form new Waller County in 1873, the location of Nelsonville was closer to the west end of the county where the highest population concentration existed. This did not materialize because when the railroads crossing the region were built they passed through Bellville, New Ulm, and newly established Kenney, not Nelsonville.

An undated letter by Karel Sula indicates that the first Czechs in the Nelsonville area were Josef Susen and Jan Mikeska who bought a farm equipped with a cotton gin. The Jan and Rosalie Coufal Silar family moved to Nelsonville in 1869, having previously lived in several communities including Post Oak Point. Most of the Germans living in this area, like most of the Czechs, were of the Protestant religion.

An early German settler was C.W.A. Ueckert, who bought the 1040 acre tract on the lower East Fork from Jasper Daniel on November 14, 1865.

In addition to the first settlers, some other early British-American family surnames of the Nelsonville community around Civil War times included Bradbury, Burns, Christoff, Dixon, Faucett, MacGregor, Bush, Nelson, Perry, Sheffield, Watson, Willis, Foster, Cole, and Scranton. Most of these families left the area in the years after the end of the Civil War. A few men married into the new Czech families and stayed, adopting the Czech culture and farming economy.

After the Civil War, the freed slaves in the area in many cases assumed their previous owner's surnames (Bonner, Houston, Flake, Burns, Daughtry, Elliott, Ward, Bethany, Shelborn). Some remained in the area, either buying their own land or working for other landowners.

An outstanding detailed description of Nelsonville's first thirty years was written by John P. Shelburne and published in the Bellville newspaper in January of 1895. The article and a photograph of the original 1838 Shelburn homestead near Blieblerville was located by O. B. Shelburne in a box of family memorabilia retained by Fairy Thompson, who was born in Nelsonville but later lived in Arkansas. The newspaper article reads as follows:

"NELSONVILLE
In the Forks of the Creek
But the
PEOPLE ARE NOT MOSSBACKS
A Thrifty, Progressive People Inhabiting
a Pretty, Productive Country

"Nelsonville is situated in the forks of East and West Mill creek, nine miles west of Bellville. It was named in honor of D.D. Nelson, who commenced the mercantile business in 1865. Nelsonville is surrounded by the finest farming land in the state. The country is well watered by East and West Mill creeks, Long branch and Beleman branch and their tributaries.

"Farming is the principal occupation of the people, for which the soil is admirably adapted. It varies from a light sandy to a jet black, the prevailing character being a rich loam. The principal fruit productions are peaches, pears, plums, figs, quinces, apples and grapes. All kinds of vegetables are raised in great profusion. The sugar cane is cultivated to great extent, from which our people make their own sugar and molasses. Among the forest trees are post oak, pin oak, pecan, hickory, black walnut, mulberry, cottonwood and a variety of others.

"The climate being tempered by the cool breeze from the gulf, is salubrious and delightful. This section is well supplied with fine drinking water, which is obtained from wells, ranging from ten to fifty feet in depth.

"In the year 1865 Mr. D. D. Nelson erected the first house here, which was a small frame building with two rooms, one of which he used for a dwelling and the other for a store. He commenced the mercantile business with a capital of about $250, with a yearly profit of about $50.

"In the year 1866 Isaac Lewis engaged in the general mercantile business, and in the following year Steuben Flake was admitted as a partner, the firm being named Lewis and Flake. About this time dwellings and other business houses were constructed, and since then the following men have engaged in the mercantile business at this place: Conorane, R. C. Burns, Cheser, Lewis and Bethany, Faucett and Lindemann, Howard and Hyman, Cristoff and Quillin, John Mikeska, Miller Bros., Newman, who afterwards admitted Joseph Cristoff as a partner, under the firm name of Newman and Cristoff; Lewis and Irvin, Joseph Irvin Jr., John Mazac, Elliot and Dunn, N. Burns, A. Pelza, Wolf and Lewis.

"Lalla and Meissner commenced business in 1882, the partnership of which firm was dissolved by the death of Lalla. Mr. Meissner then continued business alone until 1886, when he admitted a partner under the firm name of M. R. Meissner & Co., but after a period of nine months the partnership was dissolved, and Mr. Meissner again continued business alone. He is at the present time the leading merchant of this place. In 1890 Elam Lockwood engaged in the mercantile business and continued same until his death, which occurred in the latter part of the year 1893. Joseph Matejka opened up a store in the fall of 1892, and in 1893 Frank Matejka was admitted as a partner, which business is now conducted under the firm name of Matejka Bros.

"A postoffice was established here in 1873, with R. W. Thompson as postmaster. Since that time the following men have acted in that capacity: Jos. Cristoff, N. Burns, R. W. Thompson, M. R. Meissner, and Jos. Matejka. When the postoffice was first established we received the mail weekly; it was afterwards changed to tri-weekly mail, and at the present time we have a daily mail.

"In the year 1865 Dr. Cole located here and began the practice of medicine. He has been succeeded by the following men of that profession: Drs. White, R. W. Thompson, John Dixon, O. L. Williams, G. W. Foster, M. Decaussay, A. Hanka, J. C. McGregor, and W. R. P. Thompson. The last two named are now practicing under the firm name of McGregor and Thompson.

"The following are the names of men who have practiced law at this place: A. J. Bell, Jas. H. Shelburne, Jas. M. Bethany, F. E. Thompson, J. W. Willis, and the firm of Bell and Bethany.

"These are the men who have been engaged in the blacksmith business here: Charles Maynor, Switzer, Dotson, Gendreau, Hildebrant, Wischnewsky, W. R. Lee, Tom Kunak and Frank Hinza.

"The following are the names of carpenters, wood-workmen and wheelwrights: Frank Prasichek, Koch, Campbell, Meyer, Quillen, Cristoff, Brown, Pittman, Gious, Heinrich, Denaka, Mathews and Olsen.

"The following are men who have kept a meat market here: Hurdle, Walchek, Cristoff, August Meissner, Price Manly, Wm. Sanders, R. Meissner, Schaffner and Sailer.

"In 1870 Fritz Moore opened up a saddlery and harness shop, but in 1885 he closed out his business and no one has since succeeded him.

"We have had only one tinner at this place, R. Potter.

“W. A. Thompson and R. W. Thompson, residents of this place, have represented Austin county in the state legislature.

“The following are men who have served as county commissioners from this beat: Henry Smidt, Jesse Ward, Andrew Lindemann, Ernst Vogelsang, Jos. Lalla, Henry Hening, R. W. Thompson, Chas. Haedge, M. R. Meissner, and John Malechek.

“The following are the names of men who have served as justice of the peace of this precinct: D. D. Nelson, Wm. Fordtran, W. Z. Dixon, Max Meissner, Jas. H. Shelburne, F. M. Thompson, Jas. Willis, Wm. Wennenweiser, F. C. Lindemann, E. C. Ogg, John P. Shelburne, Sr., and A. W. Sailer.

“The following are the constables: W. A. Thompson, Henry Miller, S. A. Minton, J. P. Manly, Max Schaffner, and Ike Shelburne.

“In 1867 Ed Brune erected a twenty-five horse-power steam gin, grist and saw mill, it being then the only gin within the forks of Mill creek. That year he ginned 135 bales of cotton, and in 1873 he ginned 400 bales. In the same section of county during the year 1894 there has been 5,000 bales ginned, which shows what a great increase there has been in the production of the fleecy staple since 1867.

“The following is a list of the secret orders located at this place: G. W. Foster Masonic lodge, No. 306; Robt. E. Lee Chapter, No. 109; the C.S.P.S. Lodge, and the Sons of Herman.

“We have two churches here, the Methodist and the Lutheran.

“We have three good schools in this scholastic district – at Nelsonville, Oak Hill and the Nelsonville Prarie school. This year’s scholastic census shows 250 children within the scholastic age. We also have two colored schools, with 100 children in the district.

“The oldest native Texan now resides at Nelsonville in the person of Mr. Jas. Daughtry, who was born in the eastern part of Texas, July 18, 1823.

“We also claim to have one of the oldest married couples in this county. Mr. Samuel A. Shelburne and Miss Adeline J. Bell were married January 30, 1845, consequently on the 30th of this month they will celebrate their golden wedding anniversary.

“Nelsonville and the surrounding neighborhood is inhabited by an intelligent, refined and peaceable class of people. This is one of the healthiest localities in the state.

“The future prospects of our town and the surrounding country are quite flattering. We invite all people who are seeking homes to come and take a bird’s-eye view of this, the garden spot of Texas.

John P. Shelburne”

Nelsonville was a flourishing community at the turn of the century. An account of the town written in German in 1899 by Wm. A. Trenckmann in his "History of Austin County, Texas" indicates:

"Three gins clean and gin the cotton, which is produced in large quantities. Two stores supply the population with merchandise; and a place for the men to quench their thirst after a hard day's work is not lacking. In Nelsonville itself and in Oak Hill are well equipped blacksmith shops. Vsajemost Lodge of the C.S.P.S. Order owns a roomy hall in which feasts, balls and other entertainment takes place. The Fruehling Lodge, No. 112, O.D.H.S. is located here too. In Scranton Grove, in Nelsonville, and in Oak Hill are schools for white children; and in the first named settlement, where German is strongly represented, the German language is taught. Most of the young people of the area speak Czech, German and English with equal facility.

"The oldest settler is probably the respected Dr. Hanka, who moved here from New Ulm. Between Nelsonville and Scranton Grove lives one of the eldest Texans, eighty-two year old S.A. Shelborne, who came with his family as a youth in 1838 to Austin County. His father, John P. Shelborne settled on Mill Creek near present-day Blieblerville. He is still as hale and hardy as an old oak tree, and with his remarkable memory, loves to tell of olden times. Several years ago he and his equally active life companion celebrated their golden wedding anniversary in the circle of their children and grandchildren."

The following article is from the Bellville Times, April 6, 1978 "Local History – The Bellville Historical Society – The Folk of Early Nelsonville by William Lynch Fuller.

" .... One prosperous little community in the northern part of the county, Near Bellville, was founded at about the time of or immediately after the War Between the States. The first business there was owned by the Nelson family after whom the town takes its name. Up to and ever since that time, the Nelsonville area has produced and nurtured many sturdy Austin County citizens. Some of Bellville's and the county's best-known and best-loved citizens have been from Nelsonville as the following letter, sent to the Bellville Times in 1936 from Dr. Charles Foster, an old Austin County Countryman, indicates.

Dear Sir,

Wife and I made a trip to Austin County last Tuesday, 21st inst., and I fully intended to have called on you, but it was raining when we reached Bellville and I did not talk to anyone except Ed Batla, your courteous and very accommodating County Clerk, and three or four other men who happened to be in the court house at the time. We went down to Sealy with the intention of going out to San Felipe for the Centennial celebration but the rain continued until after we had finished dinner at Jack Hillboldt's Café, so we returned to Bellville, without stopping there, and went out to Nelsonville where I was born and reared until I was 17 years old when I came to Georgetown in March 1887 and we have lived in this, Williamson County, ever since.

Having been away from Austin Co. for almost fifty years, and not having visited Nelsonville for about 40 years, I was anxious to go back there and see how the old place looks, our old home, my mother's grave, etc. The new highway changes the appearance of the village almost completely and passes out old home on the south side, whereas the old road (which still runs through the town) missed our home about 200 yards to the north. Thos. M. Kamas owns and lives on our old place where he conducts the Nelsonville Garage and Filling Sta. We found Mr. Kamas and his wife very nice people and they took great pleasure in showing us about the place and extending every courtesy possible. We also found Dr. Kroulik, the only physician there, to be a very courteous and affable gentleman and he showed us where the original buildings which were there when we lived there stood, explaining other changes and furnished us with all of the information that he could. So our visit to the village of Nelsonville was quite pleasant. Having only a few minutes to stay there we went on out to the Old Thompson place at Oak Hill schoolhouse, where my mother was buried, in the family graveyard, about 64 years ago. My grandfather James Thompson settled that place in an early day. I certainly would like to know just the year. Possibly you can furnish me with this information. My mother's oldest brother, a half brother, James W. Bethany, was a large planter and a stock man at Nelsonville long before the civil war and raised a family of twelve children married and had children, two of the girls having 15 and 16 children each, so there was a large family of Bethany's. James M. Bethany, his oldest son, was states attorney of Austin Co. for many years, district attorney at the time of his death. Dr. R.W. Thompson, who was born and raised at Nelsonville and practiced medicine at Nelsonville and Bellville for many years was my mother's youngest brother.

My father came to Texas from Illinois in 1857 and settled at San Felipe where he was city secretary for some years. He taught school in Austin Co. for ten years, graduated in medicine at Tulane Univ. of La. In 1869 and practiced medicine at Nelsonville until 1887, when he moved to Georgetown where he lived until he died, Nov. 28, 1921.

My father was a great lover of Masonry and the Masonic Lodge at Nelsonville was named for him, G.W. Foster Lodge No. 306. He was also one of the charter members of Bellville Chapter, R.A.M. and acted for the Grand Master of Masons of Texas in the laying of the corner-stone of the Austin County Court House. And I am pleased to note that this court house is still in good condition. I noticed that the exterior looks well, there being only a few cracks in the walls, and they are short. Apparently the foundation, material and workmanship of this building was first class.

My mother's family being such a large family, it seemed to me when I was a boy living there that almost everybody was kinfolk of mine. And now I find none of my family there, and very few friends. 50 years makes a tremendous change in the personnel of the citizenry of any place, quite naturally.

I found my mother's grave without much trouble and tombstone and foot marker are in good condition. After cleaning them off I could read the inscriptions easily. The stones are standing perfectly plumb, which is rather remarkable considering the fact that the graveyard fence has been allowed to fall down and the cattle and other livestock in the pasture surrounding the graveyard can go in and out at will. This farm is now owned by John Moudry I am told. It is part of the old Thompson farm which belonged to my uncle, Frank Thompson, when I left Austin County. ---------

With best wishes for you and the Bellville Times, I am
Yours very truly,
Chas. C. Foster, M.D."

The "Bellville Countryman" newspaper reported in its May 29, 1861 edition: "LARGE COTTON - Last Monday Capt. A. J. Bell of Forkston showed me a stalk of cotton about three feet in height, very full of squares, with several blooms and some buds as large as bird's eggs. The Capt. Says he has about forty acres of cotton equally as good as this stalk. This specimine is decidedly the most forward we have seen".

The October 16, 1861 issue of the Bellville Countryman included: "We understand from E.W. Matthews that the cotton crop along the raod from here to Industry and New Ulm are yet white as snow banks, and that some farmers in that portionof the county will make an average crop. The army worm has been very partial in its devastating travels, while some crops would be almost entirely destroyed, an adjacent farm would yield an abundant crop".

The March 22, 1862 issue of the Bellville Countryman noted: "Married: In Forkston on the 13th inst. By Rev. David Fisher, Capt. Jasper N. Daniel to Miss Elizabeth Manley, both of Austin County".

Early Public Establishments

Church:

The Czech immigrants and their children who settled in the Nelsonville area after the Civil War were predominantly from the area around Vsetin and Zadverice, Moravia, a strong Protestant region in mostly Catholic Czech lands in the middle nineteenth century.

Before the war, Czech immigrants to Texas were also in the Protestant minority from the Cermna, Nepomuky and Voderady, Cechy, region; several of these families moved to Nelsonville in the 1860's and 1870's. The first Czech protestant church (Unity of the Brethren) in the United States was organized at Wesley, Texas, in 1866. With the continuing influx of Czech immigrants after the Civil War, a second Unity of the Brethren church was organized in Industry, Texas, in 1875 and a church built in 1879. Many of the Czech residents living in the Nelsonville area were participants in organizing this church, including Vinc P. Shiller, Joseph Heil, Sr. & Jr., John A. Shiller, Vinc Marek, Ludwig Marek, J. Jansa and Frank Maresh. The first pastor was Rev. Henry Juren (adjacent photo) who moved to Industry from Fayetville in 1879 and remained until 1892 when he moved to Wesley.

Rev. Juren was the active pastor for the protestant Czechs who lived in the Mill Creek Forks area until 1893, when a Unity of the Brethren church was built in Nelsonville.

The origins of the only church in Nelsonville are given in a booklet titled "Unity of the Brethren in Texas (1855 - 1966)", as follows: "The Unity of the Brethren Church congregation was organized at Nelsonville in 1893 by the Rev. Anton Motycka. Pastor Motycka, Iowa-born and Oberlin-educated, served both as minister and local schoolteacher. The charter membership included 27 families. The first elders were Tom Kamas, Josef Estarek, Jr., John Elsik, Josef Pechal, Josef Chlapek, Sr. and Tom Kamas of near Kenney.

A parsonage was built in 1893 and the following year a cupola steeple was added to the former school building in which the services were held. The 1900 hurricane that leveled Galveston demolished this first church. In 1902 the congregation built a new church while the Rev. Alios B. Koukol, a New York minister, was serving as pastor. In 1903 the Rev. Motycka returned from Kansas, where he continued to serve the congregation until his death in the pulpit at Industry during a confirmation service in 1935."

Post Office:

The first Post Office opened in Nelsonville in 1872, with Isaac Lewis appointed postmaster on July 8 of that year. As was typically the case in small towns, the post office was located in the mercantile store and the store owner was postmaster. Napoleon Burns was appointed postmaster on December 21, 1875, followed by J.F. Cristoff on January 14, 1876. Louise Lesikar was postmistress for a few years before about 1911.

According to Mrs. Celesta Albert Balke in her "History of Blieblerville", The first post office in Blieblerville was established in January, 1892, with Mr. Robert Bleiber as postmaster. It was located in the Bleiber combination store/saloon/living quarters and stayed in this location until 1898. Paul Albert was appointed postmaster in October of that year when he bought out Mr. Bleiber's business and built a new store. The post office in Blieblerville remained in this location until June of 1976, when the current, freestanding building was constructed. Herman Albert was postmaster from October, 1921, to February, 1936, followed by Celesta Albert Balke who served until January, 1977. Mrs. Joyce Glenwinkel Krause assumed postmaster duties in 1977.

Schools:

The first recorded schoolteacher in the area was Samuel Elliot, age 26, born in North Carolina, living with his brother Elias Elliot in 1850. It is assumed the "school" was in a house or outbuilding on the Elias Elliot plantation in the Grimes League near Nelsonville.

Several schools were in the lower forks of Mill Creek in the late 1800s and early 1900s. The County Judges Record of 1880 shows that the following public schools in the Nelsonville area received public assistance during the 1880 school year:

1. Desterweg Pestalazzi School Community #10. Fifty pupils were enrolled in July, 1880. A. G. Lindemann, C. Haedge and A. Roessler were trustees, receiving $150.00 from the County.
2. Wards Chappel School Community #24 was given $105.00 on July 22, 1880, with 35 pupils. Edmund Ward, Allen Daniel and Sam Houston were trustees. It was located in Oak Hill and attended by the black children of that area.
3. Oak Hill School Community # 36 was recognized for public funding of $120.00 on July 31, 1880, serving 40 pupils. Trustees were F. M. Thomnpson, S. G. Howard and Thomas H. Bradbury. The Oak Hill school was active from 1880 to 1947. Joseph Watson taught there in the 1880's and '90's. The 1890 Census of Union Veterans of Austin County indicates that Joseph Watson was a Private and Corporal in Company A, and a Private in Company K, 5th U.S. Artillery, ensilting on August 5, 1861 and discharged August 5, 1864.
4. Nelsonville School Community # 42 was organized on July 31, 1880, receiving $180.00 for 60 pupils. Trustees were James W. Bethany, Robert W. Thompson and George W. Foster. In 1890, the school was located on the second floor of the CSPS Hall; a dance hall occupied the first floor. Later, the public school in Nelsonville was located on the south side of today's Highway 159, followed by a move adjacent to the church on the north side of original road through the town. There were a number of teachers over the years. A Mr. Odradovsky was one of the first. Charles Soucek from Oklahoma was an early teacher at Nelsonville, marrying his student Albina Dusek before moving back to Oklahoma. Anton Motycka taught school in addition to his duties as Unity of the Brethren Church Pastor in the 1890's and early 1900's.For a period of time there were two teachers, Rev. Motycka and Miss Lotte Meissner. Miss Gardenia Matjka served as an aid to Rev. Motycka. Many of the teachers boarded with established families in the town while they were teaching. Staying with the Louis Albert family were Ervin Hammack, Lois Logan (four years) and Eunice Kamas. Staying with the Dr. John Kroulik family were, Henrietta Roensch (two years), Ollie Burns (one year), J.J. Sula (four years) and Leona Frnka (one year)
5. Nelsonville Colored School Community # 40 received $84.00 on July 31, 1880, to serve 28 pupils. Known as Salem School, Green Johnson, Nelson Flakes and Sam Friday were trustees.
6. New Bremen School Community #44 was recognized in 1880. It had 37 pupils and received $111.00 in public funds. Joseph Lala, W. Sange and John Schiller were trustees.

Scranton Hill school was active from 1872 to 1935. There was also a school in the Santa Anna community near Nelsonville.

It was not uncommon for the locations of the schools to move several times. They usually were located on the private land of an individual who had school-aged children and was willing to host the school nearby for convenience. After that landowner's children no longer attended school, the building would be moved to a new location on someone else's land. The Oak Hill, Nelsonville and New Bremen schools moves several times in this manner. Transportation limitations were of course the reason for the large number of schools. From a practical standpoint they needed to be within daily walking or horseback riding distance for the attending students. Grades one through seven or eight were the norm for these one-room schools. Those few students who went on to high school usually did so in Bellville, boarding during the week with a family living in Bellville. The distance from the Nelsonville area to Bellville, plus the uncertainty and difficulty of fording Mill Creek before the automobile and paved highway, as well as the needs of their efforts on the farm, discouraged most students from attending school past the eighth grade.

Commercial and Professional Services

The major commercial establishments in the lower forks of Mill Creek were typical of farming communities of that time. Cotton gins, mercantile stores, saloons, and later automobile garages constituted the commercial businesses. Doctors and blacksmiths provided professional services.

Seed Store:

The first commercial establishment in Nelsonville was a building owned by C. F. Helmuth of Bellville to store seeds (cotton, corn, etc.) from one year to the next. This building was demolished and in its place Tom Kamas built his original garage. Joe Motycka built a home on this location when Kamas moved to the new highway.

Cotton Gins:

In the Oak Hill area three gins were operated at various times by the Estarak, Jan Mikeska, Dolezal, Fritz Huber and Hugo Fisher families. The Hugo Fischer gin was the primary commercial operation in Oak Hill around the turn of the century. In addition to the cotton ginning equipment was a grist mill which was used by the local farmers for grinding corn into meal for cornbread.

In Nelsonville, the first gin was established in a location about one mile outside of Nelsonville toward Blieberville. Adolph Dahse was an early operator of this gin; he later sold it to Mr. Motl in the early 1920s, when he moved to operate the mercantile store in Nelsonville. After this gin closed, a Mr. Zettle opened a gin between National Cemetery and Hwy. 159.

The Wienke gin located west of the West Fork on the road from Nelsonville to New Bremen was a major commercial establishment in its day. In addition to the cotton ginning capability, Wienke provided the only sawmill in the area as well as the only molasses from sugar cane processing plant in the area. Local molasses was used as a sugar substitute by the residents. Hardwood trees (principally Pecan, Oak, Elm and some Walnut) were cut by the farmers and hauled in sections by mule or oxen to the sawmill, where the tree sections were sawed into boards which were then hauled back home to be used in building houses, barns, and other outbuildings.

The gins were powered by steam engines. Operation of the boilers to drive these gins required water and wood fuel, and produced pressurized steam which was used to drive the machinery. A steam whistle at each of these gins became a fixture in the countryside during cotton harvesting season. The whistle could be heard for miles around, and was used to indicate lunchtime to farmers in the field. Also, when the raw cotton feed for the gin was about to be depleted, the ginner would blow the whistle as a signal for farmers to bring in wagons of fresh cotton for ginning. In this manner the scheduling of the cotton harvest through the ginning process, minimizing delays of the farmers at the gin, would be regulated by the steam whistle at the gin.

Blieblerville had at least two gins, one opererated by a Mr. Whering.

Mercantile Stores:

The first mercantile store to be operated in Nelsonville was opened by David Nelson in 1865, followed by Issac Lewis in 1866. Fritz Lindemann, Faucett, and Meissner followed as owners of this early store located near the current church parsonage. Four individuals were listed as "merchants" in the 1880 Census: B. Lewis (son of Isaac), A. Wolf, Isaac Coehn, and N. Burns.

Jan H. Shiller moved to Nelsonville from Industry and opened a grocery store and dance hall with Jan Mikeska in 1873. The business lasted less than a year, as Shiller became incapacitated with illness for several months and the credit extended by the store resulted in bancruptcy when a crop failure in a drought year prevented the farmers from being able to repay their loans. Joseph Lala owned the store for a short time. Frank Matejka operated the store for several years, selling it to C.F. Hellmuth of Bellville around 1900. Helmuth Mercantile issued a number of trade tokens during this period, likely given to local farmers in place of cash payments for live chickens, milk and other farm produce sold to the store. The tokens were redeemable at the store and used to pay for purchases just like cash. Joe Jezek was the store operator for several years. The Jezek's lived in Nelsonville next to the Kroulik residence. Anton Dittert operated the store for a year, then it was purchased by Paul Albert in the early 1920s. The store was located on the old road through Nelsonville, across the street from Dr. Kroulik's office. When the new paved highway came to Nelsonville in 1929, it bypassed the town to the south by a few hundred yards. Paul Albert moved his store across the new highway to it's current location at the intersection of Hwy. 159 and Skalak Road. Louis Albert and his wife Hettie operated the store until the mid-1980's.

Adolph Dahse opened a mercantile store in Nelsonville in the early 1900's. This store was used by Walter Herring as a garage for a year around 1918. After being vacant for two years, it was reopened by Henry Maresh. This store burned down in the late 1920s.

According to Mrs. Celesta Albert Balke, Blieblerville's first mercantile store was operated by Isaac Lewis before 1892. The building was a combination store, saloon and living quarters, and was located on the west side of the road through town just south of the current post office. Robert Bleiber, who arrived in the area in 1889, owned a peddler wagon which traveled to the farms selling merchandise and buying farm products. The wagon was operated by Mr. Lutz. Apparently, Bleiber bought the original Lewis establishment aroung 1892. Paul Albert purchased Mr. Bleiber's business in 1898, and built a new store across the street. Herman Albert bought the business from his brother Paul in 1921; it later became the Casper Balke Store.

Oak Hill had one combination mercantile store / gasoline filling station operated by George Mikeska.

Doctors:

Gregor C. MacGregor was perhaps the first doctor in the area. He was born in North Carolina in 1825 and came to the area in 1851 where he married Portia Fordtran, eldest daughter of Charles and Amanda Fordtran. In the 1860 census he is listed as a wealthy farmer in the Forkston area; in 1870 his occupation is listed in the census as "doctor, farmer, medic". Before 1880 he moved to Waco and in 1882 was influential in establishing the nearby railroad town named for him – McGregor.

The grave marker of J. D. Dixon in the Dixon-Grimes Cemetery has his name engraved with the prefix "Dr." It is not known if he was a medical doctor, or, if so, if he practiced in the area. He was born in 1846 and died in 1873.

Dr. George W. Foster came to Texas fom Illinois in 1857, where he first settled at San Felipe. He graduated in Medicine from Tulane University in 1869, established a practice in Nelsonville, and married a daughter of Jane Thompson, an early settler. He moved to Georgetown from Nelsonville in 1887.

Dr. Jasper Nelson Williamson graduated from medical school and after four years of practicing medicine at Nelsonville, he practiced in Bellville, Old Travis and Cat Spring before leaving Austin County. He was the son of early settler E. C. Williamson.

In 1895 the home and office of Dr. J. C. McGregor (born 1855 in North Carolina) were located in Nelsonville on what later became the Tom Kamas residence and store.

Dr. Robert Watson Thompson was born December 12, 1842, at Nelsonville, and practiced in Nelsonville in the late 1800's, in the location on the original road through town which was later purchased by Dr. John Kroulik. He later moved to Bellville, then to Smithville. He died on May 11, 1918. His wife was Virginia Ann was born on December 20, 1847, and died June 25, 1910. Both are buried in Oak Knoll Cemetery, Bellville.

Dr. Anton Nicodem Hanka with his young wife were among the earliest settlers of New Ulm. He was born in Teplic, Czechoslovakia, in 1813, the son of Frantisek and Anna Hausenblasova Hanka. He studied in medicine and theology in Veinna and Prague, graduating in 1853. Hanka married a former nun, abandoned his Catholic faith and immigrated to America in 1854, landing in New York but promptly settling in Texas.

Most of his career of medical practice was in New Ulm. In his later years he moved to Nelsonville, where he purchased a home and continued his medical practice. Dr. Hanka died in 1904 at Nelsonville.

Dr. John Kroulik was born west of Industry in 1872, son of Jan and Frantiska Pachr Kroulik. Jan Kroulik immigrated from northeastern Bohemia in 1853. Frantiska Pachr immigrated from southwestern Moravia in 1855. John Kroulik attended school in the area, and later high school in Bellville. He attended Southwestern University in Georgetown, followed by medical school in Galveston, receiving his degree in 1897. After a short internship in Palestine, Texas, Kroulik purchased the home and business of Dr. R.W. Thompson in Nelsonville in 1897. At this time Dr. McGregor and Dr. Hanka were also practicing in Nelsonville. Dr. Kroulik practiced medicine for his entire career in Nelsonville, retiring in 1939. During much of this time the nearest hospital was in Brenham. When his patients needed surgery, Dr. Kroulik usually assisted Dr. Piers of Brenham with the operation. Dr. Bernard Knolle of Industry and Dr. J.A. Neeley of Bellville were consulted for difficult cases. The fee for delivering babies was $15 to $20, payable after the cotton crop was harvested. Dr. Kroulik filled his own prescriptions; quinine, calomel and castor oil were plentiful. He had facilities for a few simple tests like urine sugar and blood pressure; there were no nearby diagnostic laboratories.

Blacksmiths:

Jan Korenek was a blacksmith near Nelsonville. Thomas Krampota operated a shop in Nelsonville around 1918 before moving to the Kenney area. His competitor was Charles Stupka, who operated a shop near the church and school. Stupka moved to Guy in Fort Bend County, and a Mr. Wolters operated the shop in the period around 1925.

Josef Kroulik operated a blacksmith shop near the Hugo Fisher gin in Oak Hill in the 1900 - 1910 period. He then moved to Smithville where he operated a blacksmith / wheelwright shop until he retired and moved back to Oak Hill to live with the family of his daughter Sadie Kroulik Bravenec.

John Stalmach worked as a blachsmith at the shop operated by Robert Bleiber in Blieblerville.

The 1880 Census for this area lists "Aug. Mischnowsky" and "Paul Gendniar" (of Canada) as blacksmiths, and Henry Miller as a wheelwright.

Other Professional Services:

In addition to blacksmiths, several other individuals were listed in the 1880 Census with the following professional services as occupations:

E. D. Dixon and S. C. Landrum	Machinists (at gins and mills)
Wm. Baumaster	Stonemason
Paul Zapalac	Carpenter
Peter Hubbard	Painter
James W. Bethany	Lawyer

Automoblie Garages:

Walter Herring used the Dahse Store building as the first automobile garage in Nelsonville for about a year prior to his moving to Smithville. Tom Kamas was a clerk in Joe Jezek's mercantile store in the early 1920s, and established his garage during this period. Mr. Kamas moved his garage in 1929 to be located on the new highway, and built his residence adjacent to the new garage location. The store evolved to sell groceries and other merchandise: it closed when Mr. Kamas retired in the 1980's.

Saloon / Dance Hall:

The saloon and outdoor dance platform opened by Jan Shiller and Jan Mikeska in 1873 was later reopened and operated by John J. Bravenec and Ignac Cernosky. It was located just west of the Joe Jezek mercantile store. Frank Bednar was the last proprietor of the saloon before prohibition.

Newspaper:

A Czech language periodical titled "Listy poucne a vzdelavajici" was published in Nelsonville in 1897 (Reference: <u>Krásná Amerika: a Study of Texas Czechs, 1851 - 1979</u>, by Clifton Machann and James W. Mendl, Eakin Press (Austin), 1983).

Social Organizations

Nelsonville had chapters of five social organizations. Local Czechs joined the national Czech assurance organization (C.S.P.S) in 1891 and constructed a building on the west side of Skalak Road just south of the location of the Albert store today. The Nelsonville C.S.P.S. chapter dissolved in 1897 and was replaced by a similar state organization, S.P.J.S.T. On November 25, 1905, Nelsonville's SPJST Lodge #68 completed a hall which burned a few years later. Another SPJST hall, standing today, was built in 1924 just west of the C.S.P.S hall, which had been dismantled and lumber used to construct the adjacent Louis Albert home in 1922. Nelsonville also had a chapter of the Sons of Herman, and the G. W. Foster Masonic Lodge No. 306. The Woodmen of the World Burr Oak Camp No. 2899 was based at Nelsonville.

In Blieblerville, S.P.J.S.T. Lodge No. 33 was organized on June 10, 1900. Members present at the organizational meeting were Jan Schovajsa, Thomas Mikeska, Jiri Mikeska, Jan Susen, Jr., Jan Slacik, Jiri J. Mikeska, Frantisek Sisa, John K. Mikeska, Josef Mikeska, Jan Susen, Sr., Vinc Stepan, Josef Siptak, Josef Kamas and Jan Siptak. Jan Schovajsa was the first Lodge president. Meetings were held in the Paul Albert store until 1914, when a separate Lodge building was constructed. In 1915, the "Hvezda Miru" Lodge in Blieblerville had 266 members (133 men, 83 women and 50 children).

Nelsonville had its own orchestra of local musicians in the early 1900's members included Dr. John Kroulik, Adolph Dase, Frank Bednar, Joe J. Sula and Edward Bartay. The musicians would meet and play for the entertainment of themselves as well as others. Jan Uherka was the first person to teach music and voice in his home at Nelsonville.

Later teachers of music included the Motycka brothers, Frank Bednar and several Stalmachs. Miranda Logan was the first pupil in Nelsonville of music teacher Lydia Stalmach Maresh, who began giving piano lessons at age 18. There were monthly dances at the Nelsonville CSPS Hall. Hettie Albert recalled picking cotton all day, then rushing to clean up and go the the Saturday night dance in Nelsonville.

Life in the Nelsonville area was typical of farming communities of the times. Before the Civil War, most of the population was engaged in farming on large plantations. Cotton was the main cash crop. Sugar cane was grown for molasses, and tobacco for personal consumption. The white settlers from the older southern states who moved to Texas brought their slaves, or purchased them in Texas. The 1860 Census records shows large sums of personal property, which usually reflected the market value of the slaves. The two sons (W. L. and B. W.) of plantation owner I. Bonner had the occupation of "overseer" in 1860. After the war, many black families appear in the 1870 census for the first time by specific name, in many cases that of their former owners. Early farmers supplemented their crops with abundant wild game like deer, rabbits, turkeys and waterfowl. Hogs also roamed wild in the woods and were hunted as game for food. Cotton remained the primary cash crop of the farmers well into the twentieth century, declining after 1950. Vegetables were grown in gardens for home consumption. Farm animals included cattle for beef and milk, hogs, and some sheep and goats. Horses and mules were used for transportation and to pull buggies and wagons. These plus oxen (trained cattle) were used to pull plows to cultivate the fields. Chickens, turkeys, guineas and some ducks and geese were raised for home consumption and sale. Some farmers with marginal land fertility for cotton farming raised turkeys as their primary cash crop.

No mechanical refrigeration was available until after electricity arrived in the 1940's. Meat was eaten fresh or prepared for storage by smoking or curing. Cool water from springs was used in "spring houses" for short term storage of dairy products. Many beef clubs were formed by the farmers as an efficient means of providing fresh meat. Members of the clubs would take turns butchering a calf and sharing the cuts of meat among all members. Friday afternoons or Saturday mornings of each week were usually the time the clubs would butcher. A Uhrik of Nelsonville raised sheep and would butcher one on Wednesday's. Before that, Fisher of New Bremen would butcher in the middle of the week and deliver the fresh meat to Nelsonville. Henry Bartay made molasses from sugar cane for sale in the area mercantile stores.

The mercantile stores in the area provided a central focal point for the farmers to obtain those items they could not raise for themselves. Flour, sugar and coffee were food staples. Merchandise included hardware, pots and pans and other cooking and kitchen utensils. Shoes and cloth was a standard commodity, as weaving was not commonly practiced by the farmers. Essentially all clothes were hand made. Ready-made dresses and other clothing were rarely purchased.

In addition to being a source of goods, the stores also provided the farmers with an outlet for products from their operations. Many farmers kept dairy cattle which they milked, keeping the milk for home use and selling cream twice a week to the nearest mercantile store, where it was sent to Brenham, New Ulm or Bellville to a creamery for further processing. The stores also had a large cage or "coop" for storing live chickens which the farmers bring to the store for sale. These chickens would then be sent live to larger towns like Bellville for marketing, since there was no practical refrigeration. Chickens were a source of ready cash for the farmers; when they had no money they could always catch a chicken to use to buy staples at the mercantile store. Eggs were sold to the stores for transfer to larger markets in a similar fashion, as was sausage or "head cheese". Another source of cash for the farmers was animal skins which they trapped in the winter and sold at the mercantile store. The town of Bellville provided the largest nearby market, but some farmers took their goods to New Ulm and Kenney for sale, where the railroads provided access to markets in Houston and other cities.

The telephone came to Nelsonville in the first decade of the twentieth century. Party lines were the norm, with six or seven families on each line. Each party had its own distinctive series of rings. As the local doctor, John Kroulik was on seven different party lines to allow his patients easy access if they had a medical emergency. This resulted in much ringing of the telephone at the Kroulik residence, and put them in the position of operating a switchboard connecting two individuals on different party lines.

Electricity was first used in Nelsonville when Tom Kamas installed a generator at his place of business around 1927. Wires were run up the hill to Dr. Kroulik's home and office from the Kamas garage. Later, the Rural Electrification Administration brought commercial power to the Nelsonville area farmers and businesses in the 1940's.

Among the first owners of automobiles in the area (in the mid-1920's) were Henry Bartay and Travis Davis of New Bremen . Joe Jezek of Nelsonville owned a Maxwell.

The paved highway from Bellville to Industry was completed in Nelsonville in 1929. It generally followed the old dirt road, but made several departures to make it straighter or less expensive to build, including a detour around the town of Nelsonville. This bypass caused local businesses like the Tom Kamas garage and the Louis Albert mercantile store to relocate from the original road to the new highway several hundred yards south.

Large families were the norm for the farm families in the area, which ultimately resulted in a land shortage in the area. In the early part of the 1900's, the second generation of Czech settlers in the area grew to maturity and sought their own farms. Many moved to other less densely settled parts of the state to establish their farms. The newer Czech communities at or near Sealy, Wallis, El Campo, Caldwell and others, often had families who moved there from the Nelsonville area. A particularly large group of related families (Shiller's , Bravenec's, Lala's and Fisher's from the Oak Hill/New Bremen area) moved to Victoria County and settled near Placido, Da Costa and Guadalupe. The area they settled developed into what is today known as the Shillerville community. The cemetery in Shillerville has a state historical marker, indicating that the first families came in 1894, with Jan Shiller as their leader. This was the Jan Shiller who lived in Nelsonville and operated a mercantile store for a short period. Surnames in the

Shillerville cemetery include Balusek, Bravenec, Dusek, Faltsek, Hosek, Januta, Jirasek, Lala, Lesikar, Marek, Mikeska, Shiller, Sumbera, and Wokaty.

The memoirs of Jan Ustynik are published in the book "Czech Voices", by Clinton Machann and James W. Mendl, Jr. Ustynik writes of the return of he and his brother to Texas following the Civil War:

"On June 27, 1865, we arrived in Cat Spring, and the joy of our parents cannot be described, especially that of my mother. A big celebration was planned for the fourth of July, to commemmorate the Union victory. That was the first time I had taken part in such a party. I was twenty-three years old, and my brother was twenty-one. There were many Germans and some Czechs at the celebration. Soon after that, my mother and ten-year-old sister got sick. My sister died two days later, and my mother passed away two days after my sister. We had been home barely a month, and now father remained with us two sons and my twenty-five-year-old married sister. I also came down with influenza and suffered with it for three months.

"In August, my sister and her husband moved to Nelsonville, and my father began to pine for my mother and sister. I cooked for my father, but food had lost its flavor for him. I knew that he would rather have a woman cooking for him, so I told him that I was going away. He agreed with my decision. I took my clothes, which weren't worth much more than five dollars, and my horse and saddle. I had seventy dollars in ready cash. Father wanted the money that I had saved in Mexico, but I didn't give it to him. I rode horseback to my brother-in-law's in Nelsonville. I kept myself busy with cotton and did some carpentry work until Christmas, making about forty dollars. I rented fourteen acres for three dollars an acre and bought a pair of oxen, a plow, some corn, and hay before all my money was gone. I had to pay my brother-in-law fifty dollars a year for board. In the meantime my brother had also left my father and was in the service of Mr. Susen in Nelsonville. Now my father called for me.

"I went to him, and I was amazed at the way he had changed in the short time since mother had died. His mind was a little unbalanced. He wanted me to sell the farm because he couldn't live there anymore. He wanted to live with us. I promised him that I would oblige him. I went around to see a neighbor and offered him the fifty-acre farm for $500. Father had some cattle, and the neighbor wanted them added into the bargain. Father agreed, sold the farm, and moved to Nelsonville. That was in January of 1866. Father and I stayed with my brother-in-law that year. Father sold three bales of cotton in Brenham for $400. From that sum he kept $100 and gave $100 to me, my brother, and my sister. He pined away the whole year. I paid for my board for the year, bought some clothes, and was penniless once again. Brother got married in January of 1867, and, along with father, bought a farm from the Susens in Nelsonville for $900. I worked in a field in 1866, and got $180 for cotton, $50 for corn, and $15 for millet, $60 for the oxen, and $16 for the plow. From that money I paid my rent and other debts, and had $200 left. In 1867, I went to work for Petr Mikeska for fourteen months. My pay was $270. In 1868, I worked in carpentry and in the fall at W. Fotrama's gin five miles from Wesley. In 1869, I worked at the gin that Mr. Cole rented near Nelsonville. The job lasted four months and I made $160. In 1870, my eye hurt all year, and the doctor's bill and cost of the medicinal baths was $200, but my eye got better. In 1871, I went to work for Mr. J. W. Bethany in Nelsonville. He had a steam gin, saw, and mill, and I had to see that it was working properly. For that I got $500 a year, as well as my board, laundry, and a room. I did that for two years and six months.

"In 1873, I got married, taking for my wife Vincenc Siller's eighteen-year-old daughter, who had been born in Industry. Her parents were from Cermna in Bohemia, and from there they migrated to Moravia, and then to Texas. I rented the mill from Mr. Bethany on halves, and everything went well for us. That year my wife was very homesick, but she recovered and gave me the gift of a son. In 1874, I moved to my father-in-law's place in Industry."

Another memoir in the book "Czech Voices" is by Jan Horak, who writes "So in 1870, when I went to work for Jos. Lastovica, I gave up and married Miss Apolena Zapalacova, the daughter of Jan Zapalac from Hrozenkov, who had come to America in 1855. We rented a place from the Zapalaces near Oak Hill. We were there until 1918. The first (fraternal) organization was evangelical and came in 1874. Then a Catholic priest and some sisters came, and now English must be taught, as required by law. We had five daughters, who are maried and live in Columbus, West, Crosby, Needville and Garwood. We took in an orphan from the orphanage and adopted him. In 1918 we bought as piece of land near Fayetteville, and since then, we have farmed here."

An interesting account of life in Nelsonville at the turn of the century is given in the memoirs of Joe F. Mikolaj printed in Vestnik, July 18, 1990:

"In the beginning of the 1900's, we had no electric lights, power, autos, telephones, refrigerators, air conditioning, etc. For lights, we used candles, kerosene lamps and lanterns. Horses and mules provided travel by riding, wagon, buggy and surry. The surry was a two-seated carriage with a fringed flat top; only dirt roads which in rainy weather were almost impossible to travel.

The Lindemann's Store, at Industry, catered to the farmers with a large long wagon loaded down with drygoods, groceries, etc. drawn by six horses or mules. The sides of the wagon opened to make counters.

If there was a shortage of money, chickens, ducks and geese would be taken and placed in cages on the back of the wagon.

Soda crackers (about 4 inches square) came in tin or wooden boxes (12" X 12" X 18").

Daily, my grandmother would give us children the crackers, apples and popcorn. It was something like Cracker Jack and on the boxes was a picture of two monkeys.

A large upstairs room was used as a chapel in the home. My grandfather built an alter with a statue of the Blessed Mother as a centerpiece. At times, when weather permitted, a priest, from Sealy, would come to conduct Mass.

Uncle Frank or Uncle Joe, on horseback, would notify the members that a Holy Mass would be held at the Svajda's home.

There were no telephones at that time. Large wood cabinet wall telephones were later installed which had a crank on the side. Every member's home had a different ring; short, long, or a combination of both, as the crank was rotated; no private lines, so anyone picking up the receiver could listen in on your conversation.

On the wall of the living room, just below the chapel room, were two large cold-framed pictures of Franz Joseph and his Queen, the rulers of Austria - Hungary which at that time included Czechoslovakia.

Butcher clubs were popular in those days. Once a month, a member would butcher a beef and members came to get certain parts of the meat. Records were kept and all members in time would receive all the parts.

Since there were no refrigerators, all perishable foods were placed into containers and lowered down into a well; then came about a three-shelf metal stand, the top was a tray with water that would saturate a sheet-like cloth around the stand of shelves for food.

The first autos were the Model "T" Ford cars which cost in the $600 range and the Chevrolet 490 Model; joke of that car was -- "four days on the road and 90 days in the repair shop", usually a blacksmith shop. They also had installed the first hand-operated gasoline pumps.

In the horse era it took us all day to make it to Grandfather Mikolaj's at Fayetteville. A large lap robe was used for cover. Usually during vegitation times, the horses would have problems.

The price of cotton was 5 cents per pound in the early 1900's.

My wife, Lillie Janosky, was also born at Nelsonville a short distance from the Svajda's home. After a four-year courtship, we married in the Catholic Church in Industry."

A number of cemeteries were used over the years by the families and ethnic groups in the area. The Austin County Historical Commission published a book titled "The Cemeteries of Austin County, Texas", which lists data from most cemeteries in the county. All known cemetery records in the Nelsonville area are included in Appendix I. Additional cemeteries have been rediscovered since this book was published, notably those containing the graves of settlers of the Shelburne family.

Nelsonville Area Families after 1870

Bravenec: Jan Bravenec was born in Katerinice, Moravia, in 1842. His father Tomas and grandfather Jiri were farmers, living in House No. 115 in Katerinice. Jan married Anna Marek of Mikuluvka, Moravia. They lived on the edge of a large forest, in which Jan was employed as the equivalent of a game and forest warden. They had five sons between 1870 and 1880, two of whom died young. The family, including sons John J., Thomas and Stephen, was granted a passport on October 14, 1880, and they left for America, arriving in Galveston in December, 1880. They settled in Nelsonville, where

Jan worked as a farm laborer for several years, saving money to buy their own farm. Two daughters, Anna and Albina, were born in Nelsonville, as was another son who died young. They bought 247 acres near Oak Hill in 1891, building a house shortly thereafter. Thomas bought land and farmed in the forks of Mill Creek near their juncture below Oak Hill. Stephen bought land adjacent to his parents after he married Frances Shiller, daughter of neighboring farmer Wincent "Sam" Shiller. John J. married Louise Janacek and operated a business in Nelsonville for a period, then moved across the West Fork of Mill Creek to a farm near New Bremen. Thomas and his family farmed nearby. Anna and husband Herman Krause lived on the original Bravenec homestead. Albina married Emil Ueckert.

Shiller: The Silar (later spelled with several variations, Shiller being the most common) family origins dating back to at least 1630 are from the Cermna area in Northeastern Cechy (Bohemia) near the Moravian border. Nearby towns in addition to Cermna include Nepomuky, Horniho Tresnovice, Albrectice. Most of the Silars were farmers, weavers or laborers.

Vojtech Balcar, father of Johana Balcar Silar, migrated to Cermna from the mountainous country near Jamne. He was one of the charter members of the Protestant church organized in Cermna. Members met in his home in the winter and in his barn in the summer until their church was built. Johana Balcar Silar and her husband Pavel lived in House No. 3 in Nepomuky. After Pavel died, she moved with her son Josef to Albrectice in 1849. In preparation for immigration to Texas, Johana sold the house to her sister-in-law Anna Silar Jirasek, where it remained for several generations. Johana, as a partially blind elderly widow in 1851, led the first group of Czech settlers to Texas, including seven of her eight children and their families. About half died on the four month journey (overseas on the bark MARIA) before reaching Cat Spring in Austin County. Johana died upon arrival in Houston and is believed buried in an unmarked grave in the old City Cemetery on Buffalo Bayou near downtown Houston.

Wincent Samuel Shiller immigrated with his parents from Bohemia on the bark SUWA in 1853. He was four years old at that time. Their family settled first in Colorado County. His father Frantisek was last member of the large family group of Shillers who immigrated in 1851; his mother was Johana Balcar Silar.

The Shillers were strongly opposed to slavery, and suffered during the Civil War because of their beliefs. Wincent's father Frantisek Shiller died about 1865, rumored to have been murdered by Confederate Army conscriptors searching for Czech's hidden by Shiller. His widow and her children continued farming, moving to Austin Co. in 1873, when they bought 311 acres of land between Nelsonville and Oak Hill. Several of the Shiller children and some of their Bravenec neighbors and relatives moved to Victoria County (Placido /Guadalupe/ DaCosta area) in the early 1900's, responding to offers of low cost land to farm and raise their families. Frances Shiller remained behind with her husband Steven Bravenec, both of her parents, and her younger brothers and sisters.

Kroulik: The Kroulik family was originally from the northeastern Cechy (Bohemia) towns of Dzbanov and Voderady, near Litomysl. The early Krouliks were of the Protestant religion, belonging to the Evangelical Assembly in Sloupnice that was organized in the year 1782. Jan Kroulik was born in 1837 in Voderady (House #45) near Litomysl, son of Frantisek and Anna Pavlicek Kroulik. In 1853 he emigrated with his widowed mother and his sister Anna and her husband Vaclav Janecek. His nephew Jan Janecek was born on the voyage at sea. Their ship, the SUWA, left the port of Bremen, Germany, in October, arriving at Galveston on December 24, 1853. The Krouliks went by boat to Houston, then by ox cart to Austin County. Anna Kroulik and Vaclav Janecek purchased land (about 80 acres) in the Schoenau community near Industry. They farmed, raising cotton, corn and other crops. Jan Kroulik also worked as a teamster, providing moving and delivery services to supplement his farming income. Vaclav Janecek was a tailor as well as a farmer and a teamster. He and his wife bought a farm near New Bremen in 1865, later selling it to his son and moving to near Nelsonville in 1883. Kroulik obtained his citizenship in 1859 in Bellville. He was an early member of the Wesley Brethren Church, the first Czech Protestant church established in Texas, in 1866.

On June 17, 1862, Jan Kroulik was conscripted and inducted into the Confederate Army in Austin County by Captain H. Wickeland into Company D, Infantry Battalion, Waul's Texas Legion. He was captured in the Battle of Vicksburg, released by the Union Army, and returned to his farm in Schoenau where he had to remain in hiding until the end of the war to avoid being forced into the Confederate Army a second time. He married Frantiska Pachr; they had nine children. Son John Kroulik moved to Nelsonville in 1897, where he maintained a practice as a phisician. Son Joseph Kroulik married Anna Janecek, living for several years in Oak Hill where he was a blacksmith before moving to Smithville where he owned and operated a blacksmith and wheelwirght shop.

Krause: Herman Krause immigrated from Germany with his family in 1870 when he was about ten years old. The Krause family settled between Nelsonville and Industry. Herman married Therezie Shiller, sister of Wincent S. Shiller. Their first son Herman, born in 1883, married Annie Bravenec and in 1912 bought 103 acres near Oak Hill from his father-in-law Jan Bravenec's heirs. He later bought an adjacent 50 acre tract from Angelo Holman.

Stalmach: John Stalmach, at age 17 in 1878, immigrated with his brother from the Zadverice, Moravia, area. He settled in Nelsonville, first working at Mr. Bleiber's blacksmith shop. He married Theresia Lesikar; they had six sons and two daughters. According to his daughter Lydia, he was quiet and joking, she was the family manager. He liked to work in the blacksmith shop. Their house was full of laughter and music. Valuing education, they vowed to send all eight children to college, giving them $350 each at first, with more to come if they stayed in school. Their homestead was a log house near New Bremen, moving later to a farm about a mile from Nelsonville. Mr. Stalmach loved music, playing the piano, organ, mandolin, etc. One Stalmach son gave coronet lessons and played as a professional musician in a band.

Maresh: The Maresh (originally Mares) family origins are in the Lanskroun district of northeastern Bohemia (Czech Republic), principally the town of Cermna. Noted historian Frank Silar provided a genealogy of this family tracing their roots back to 1530. The original family surname was Sovaty. It was changed in the 1600s to Mares, derived from the baptismal name Martin. Members of the Mares family were among the first groups of Czech settlers to migrate to Texas. Josef Mares, his wife Theresa (nee Silar) and children Vincenc and Frantiska came on the sailing ship MARIA in 1851 with a large group of Theresa's siblings. Josef and Frantiska are known to have died before reaching Austin County. The fate of Theresa and Vincenc is unknown.

In 1853 on the SUWA with the second large group of Czechs to migrate to Texas were Josef and Anna Haisler Mares of Nepomuky near Cermna and their children Rosalia, Josef, Vincenc, Theresa, Frantisek and Frantiska. They settled in Austin County.

Anna, the eldest daughter of Josef and Anna Haisler Mares, had married distant relative John Mares in 1852, staying in Cermna until 1867 when they also moved with their family to Texas, sailing on the bark Texas from Bremen and arriving in Galveston on December 14. They settled in Austin County and bought a farm between the Schoenau community and Industry in 1869. In 1883 John, Anna and their unmarried children moved to near Nelsonville, buying a farm in the Scranton Grove community. Their two sons William and Joseph each bought a portion of the Maresh homestead and raised their families on these farms.

Stepan: The first members of the Stepan family immigrated to Texas from Hostalkove, near Vsetin in eastern Moravia (Czech Republic). Martin Stepan and his family came with a larger group of Moravians from the same region, departing Bremen on the sailing ship VON VIENEKE on April 24, 1855 and arriving in Galveston on June 14, 1855. A passenger list printed in a German newspaper (the *Allgemeine Auswanderer Zeitung*, July 30, 1855) for the VON VIENEKE includes Martin Stepan plus 3 family members (his first wife and two children). The Stepans traveled by ox cart to Cat Spring, where they lived temporarily while Martin found work splitting rails. Shortly after their arrival in Cat Spring in 1855, their daughter and then Mrs. Stepan died of yellow fever. Martin Stepan then married Rozina Zapalac who with her parents and siblings had also came from Moravia to Texas on the VON VIENEKE. Martin and Rozina settled in a Ross Prairie community called Pisek close to Ellinger in Fayette County. Martin worked for about ten years as a day laborer splitting rails and later working near Frelsburg at a saw mill. He applied for U.S. citizenship in Fayette County on October 13, 1860, and again in Austin County on February 9, 1876. Around 1865 he bought a farm near Ellinger, then sold it and moved around 1870 to Austin County, purchasing a farm near Blieblerville where he and Rozina lived for the remainder of their lives.

Rosina Stepan, a sister of Martin Stepan and wife of Steve Slovak, came with her family to Texas in 1877 and settled near Blieblerville either on or next to the farm owned by Martin Stepan. Stepan (Steve) Stepan, probably a nephew of Martin, immigrated in 1880, married Anna Marek before 1892 and ultimately settled in Kovar, Bastrop County, Texas.

Land Grant from State of Coahuila and Texas to Stephen F. Austin

Original dated January 15, 1830 is located in the archives of the Land Commission of Texas in Austin. The document is penned in Spanish and is translated as follows:

"Honorable Commissioner General:

"I, Empresario Stephen F. Austin, with due respect declare to you: That I have introduced more than 100 families, part of my contract of colonization for 500 families made with the Government of the State of Coahuila and Texas on the 4th of June of the year of 1825, as shown by the list of names of said families and other particulars relative to the matter which exist in the Archives of this Colony to which I refer. Therefore, by virtue of the right conceded by my aforesaid contract and of the Law of Colonization of the 24th of March of 1825, I ask you please, as Commissioner General for the distribution of lands and the issuing of titles, to put me in possession of five leagues and five labors which correspond to me by my said contract for each one hundred families that I introduce and to issue to me the corresponding title of possession for the said five leagues and five labors as part of the premium which is allowed to me by virtue of my aforesaid contract.

"I have chosen four leagues and four labors of the aforesaid five on the forks of Palmito Creek, known in English by the name of Mill Creek, situated about 8 leagues, more or less northwest of this Town and adjoining the two branches of the aforesaid Creek and lands of Samuel M. Williams and Benjamin Eaton."

The document goes on to include selection of the fifth league and labor adjacent to the town of San Felipe de Austin, and the Mexican Government granting title to the land to Austin, and concludes as follows:

"Therefore, I beg you please to do as I have asked above in order that I may obtain my rights in conformity with the law and my aforesaid contract.

"Town of Austin, 28th of December of 1829.

"Estevan F. Austin

(Rubric)"

In the margin of this document Austin amends: "Moreover: The tract which I have requested having been surveyed by the Surveyor in the forks of Palmito Creek, only four leagues result, and it is impossible to add to them the four labors because all the adjoining tract is occupied, and therefore, I solicit the said labors in another location…" The remainder of the margin note describes the desired four labors near San Felipe, and concludes with Austin's signature. The land title is then conveyed to Austin:

"CITIZEN JUAN ANTONIO PADILLA, Commissioner General of the Supreme Government of the State of Coahuila and Texas for the distribution of vacant lands of the same state: Whereas Citizen Estevan F. Austin as Empreassario has introduced and established 150 families with the circumstances required by the law in fulfillment of his contract for 500 families with the Supreme Government of the State of the 4th of June of 1825, and as is agreed by Article 3 of the Contract that said Empresario shall receive as premium 5 leagues and 5 labors in conformity with the provisions of Article 12 of the law, I, the Commissioner General, exercising the powers vested in me, and in the name of the State, concede to, confer upon, and put him in real and personal possession of five leagues and five labors of the class and quality prescribed by law as the premium corresponding to 100 families of the larger number which he has already introduced and established in the country within the limits of his contract; said tract is surveyed by the Surveyor, Horace Chrisman, previously appointed for the purpose, within the following situations and boundaries, to wit: Four leagues are situated on the forks of Palmito Creek, known in English by the name of Mill Creek, about 8 leagues a little more or less northwest of the Town of San Felipe de Austin, the survey of which was begun at the lower corner of the tract of Samuel M. Williams, which is situated on the east margin of the west branch of said Palmito Creek and at a distance of 10 varas from a pin oak bearing north 28^0 east marked A and 4 varas from another oak of the same species bearing 40^0 east marked G; from said corner said Surveyor ran a line north 43^0 east 6135 varas following the boundary of the tract of said Williams to a landmark of the same; and thence south 47^0 east he ran another line 7510 varas following the southwest boundary of the tract chosen by John Hodge and the widow Kuykendall and to the northwest boundary of the league of Benjamin Eaton; thence south 43^0 west he ran a line 1231 varas following the boundary of Eaton to his west corner and thence south 47^0 east 4000 varas following the southwest boundary of Eaton to the west corner to the corner of the league chosen by George Grimes, and thence south 47^0 east 5640 varas following the southeast boundary of Grimes to his east corner, situated on the west margin of the east branch of said Palmito Creek, and thence following the meanders of said branch downward to the junction of this branch with the west branch; and from the same junction following the meanders of said west branch upward to the place where the survey began at the south corner of the league of the aforesaid Williams, comprising within said limits the amount of one hundred million square varas in superficies, the equivalent of four leagues." (The remainder of this portion describes the metes and bounds of the fifth league and the five labors completing this grant.) "Therefore, exercising the power vested in me by the same law and consequent instructions, I issue the present instrument and order the testimonio taken from it and delivered to the interested party in order that he may possess and enjoy the tract, he, his children, heirs, and successors, or whomever from him or from them shall have cause or right. It is given in the Town of San Felipe de Austin on the 15th of January of 1830, which I sign with attendant witnesses according to the law." The document was signed by J. Antonio Padilla and witnessed by Samuel M. Williams and T. Jefferson Chambers.

2091

SELLO TERCERO — DOS REALES.

Para los años de mil ochocientos veinte y seis y ochocientos veinte y siete. ocho y nueve

Habilitado

Sr. Comisionado General

S. Felipe de Austin 28 de Diciem.e de 1829.

Al Ayuntam.to de esta villa, para que se sirva informar á continuacion, si José Sandoval, á q.n se concedió el sitio de tierra de que habla esta representacion, há cumplido con el deber que le impuso el art.o 22 de la Ley de colonizacion de 24 de Marzo de 1825.

Padilla

El Empresario Estevan F. Austin con el debido respeto ante V. hago presente: Que he introducido mas de cien familias parte de mi contrato sobre colonizacion para quinientas familias, celebrado con el Gob.no del Estado de Coahuila y Texas 4 de Junio del año de 18.. como consta la lista nominal de dichas familias, y demas particulares sobre la materia que obran en el Archivo de esta Colonia a que me refiero. En virtud pues del derecho q.e me concede mi referido contrato y de la Ley de Colonizacion de 24 de Marzo de 1825 pido que se sirva V. como Comisionado Gral. para repartir tierras, y expedir titulos, ponerme en posesion de cinco sitios y cinco labores que me corresponden por la citada ley y mi citado contrato por dichas cien familias que introduje, y que se me expida el correspondiente titulo de posesion para

2092

otro si.
Habiendose medido con el Agrimensor las tierras que he pedido en las puntas del arroyo Caluda resultan solo quarto Cuatro Sitios los que deberan agregarse a ellos las cuatro labores a cuenta no corresponda todo el terreno colindante y por lo mismo pido las dichas quatro [illegible] como en el campante [illegible] dicho dos sitios el margen occidental del Rio de los Brazos comprendido por el No. 8 [illegible] por el No. 10 [illegible] de la Villa de San Felipe de Austin y las otras dos [illegible] No. 10 y las [illegible] 9 concedido [illegible] y [illegible] la labor No. 4 sobre el margen occidental del dicho Rio [illegible] de la dicha Villa y [illegible] del Camino Nacional [illegible] de la dicha [illegible] el citio colindante con las tierras de la dicha Villa de San Felipe de Austin
Villa de Austin [illegible] 1830

[illegible]

los dichos Cinco sitios y cinco labores Como parte del premio que me Corresponde en virtud de mi referido Contrato.

He Elegido Cuatro sitios, y cuatro labores de los referidos Cinco en las puntas del arroyo Tal[illegible] conocido en Ingles por el nombre de Mill Creek situados Cosa de ocho leguas mas o menos rumbo Nord Oeste de esta Villa y Colindando por los dos [illegible] del referido Arroyo y por tierras de Samuel M. Williams, y Benjamin Eaton. El otro sitio y labor para Completar los cinco he escogido sobre el margen occidental del Rio de los Brazos, entre las tierras de la Villa de San Felipe de Austin, y la Hacienda Concedida a James Cummings, hijo de Dona Rebeca, lindando por el Norte Con la dicha Hacienda, por el Este Con el Rio de los Brazos, por el Sur Con el lindero [illegible] de las tierras de la dicha Villa, por el poniente Con tierras baldias, estando este ultimo sitio el mismo que se concedio a [illegible] el dia 31 del mes de Agosto del año de 1825 Cuyo sitio queda [illegible] por haberse el dicho [illegible] faltado en [illegible] el primer plazo del [illegible] del Contrato segun la ley y por falta de otros requisitos legales que requiere la ley [illegible] [illegible]

B

por tanto

A. V. pido se sirva hacer como dejo referido para que reciba mi derecho de conformidad con la ley y de mi contrato mencionado.

Villa de Austin 28 de Dic.e de 1829

Estevan F. Austin

Señor Comisionado General

En consecuencia del decreto de V. que antecede en que V. se ha servido pedir de este Ayuntamiento informe si José Sandoval a quien se concedió el sitio de tierra á que habla la representacion del C. Empresario Estevan F. Austin, tiene este Ayuntam.to á decir que el citado Sandoval ni por sí ni por apoderado ó agente jamas ha pagado ning.a cantidad de dinero á este Ayuntamiento como queda prevenido por el art.o 22 de la ley de Colonizacion de este Estado, ni tampoco ha cultivado ó poblado el sitio de tierra referido, ni tampoco sabe este Ayuntamiento en donde ahora se halle el citado Sandoval

2094

SELLO TERCERO — **DOS REALES.**

Para los años de mil ochocientos veinte y seis y ochocientos veinte y siete. ocho y nueve

Lo que tiene el Ayuntamto. que responder en Contestacion al Citado decreto de V. Señor de hoy

Villa de Sanfelipe de Austin 23 de Dicie. de 1829

J. White

Samuel M Williams
Secr.

Visto el informe del Ayuntam.to de esta municipalidad, por consequencia de la falta de quantos... el Sor. José de Sandoval, y de conformidad con el Articulo 23 de la Ley de Colonizacion ... Yo Juan Antonio Padilla Comisionado General para el reparto de tierras ... de dicha Ley, ... que ... Villa de Austin ... del Cuid.o ...

Villa de Austin 7 de Enero de 1830

J. A. Padilla

D

Friedrich Ernst's Letter Encouraging German Immigration

This letter was sent from Ernst's new home in Texas to friends in Germany describing his journey to Texas and the living conditions he was experiencing. This letter was published in a newspaper and widely circulated. Through this letter and by other means Ernst is credited with attracting the first groups of Germans to join him in settling Texas.

Settlement on Mill Creek, in Austin's Colony,
State of Texas, Republic of Mexico
February 1, 1832

In February of the previous year we embarked on a brig to New Orleans. It was still winter on our departure from New York, then mild spring breezes blew upon us for four days after our departure. Between Cuba and Florida, we had later real summer, and the whole sea voyage of a thousand miles over that part of the ocean, through the Bahama Islands, into the Gulf of Mexico, up to the mouth of the Mississippi, we lay constantly against the wind and came somewhat back. On the Mississippi up to New Orleans, a hundred and twenty miles (five make a German mile) we received favorable news of Austin's Colony in Texas; we embarked again in the schooner of thirty-seven tons and landed after an eight day voyage at Harrisburgh in this colony.

Each immigrant who wishes to engage in farming receives a league of land; a single person, one-quarter of a league. A league of land contains four thousand four hundred forty acres of land, mountain and valley, woods and meadows, cut through by brooks.

The ground is hilly and alternates with forest and natural grass plains. Various kinds of trees. Climate like that of Sicily. The soil needs no fertilizer. Almost constant east wind. No winter – almost like March in Germany. Bees, birds and butterflies the whole winter through. A cow with a calf costs ten dollars. Planters who have seven hundred head of cattle are common. Principal products: tobacco, rice, Indigo grow wild; sweet potatoes, melons of an especial goodness, watermelons, wheat, rye, vegetables of all kinds; peaches of great quantity grow wild in the woods, mulberries, many kinds of walnuts, wild plums, persimmons sweet as honey; wine in great quantity but not of a particular taste; honey is found chiefly in hollow trees. Birds of all kinds, from pelicans to hummingbirds. Wild prey such as deer, bears, raccoons, wild turkeys, geese. partridges (the latter as large a domestic fowls) in quantity. Free hunting and fishing. Wild horses and buffalo in hordes; wolves, but of a feeble kind; also panthers and leopards, of which there is no danger; rich game, delicious roasts. Meadows with the most charming flowers. Many snakes, also rattlesnakes; each planter knows safe means against them.

English the ruling speech. Clothing and shoes very dear. Each settler builds … a blockhouse. The more children the better for … field labor. Scarcely three months work a year. No need for money, free exercise of religion and the best markets for all products at the Mexican harbors; up the river there is much silver, but there are still Indian races there.

We men satisfy ourselves with hunting and horse races.

On account of the yellow fever, one should arrive some weeks before the month of July or after the first of October. It is a good thing if one can speak English; only enough money is needed as is necessary to purchase a league of land. A father of a family must remember that he receives on his arrival, through the land granted to him, a small kingdom which will come to be worth in a short time from seven to eight hundred (dollars), for which it is often sold here. The expenses for the land need not be paid immediately. Many raise the money from their cattle.

Your friend,
Friedrich Ernst

N.B. Passports are not necessary. Sons over seventeen have like part in the settlement of the land.

Joseph Bergmann's Letter Encouraging Czech Immigration

The following is a translation of the first letter of Joseph Bergmann to be published in "Moravsky Noviny" newspaper in Cechy. It was sent to Albert Blaha by Wolfgang Berndt, a descendent of Mrs. Bergmann who has written articles on Bergmann in Czechoslovakia. Blaha translated the original draft of the letter, sending it to John Kroulik for editing on 6 FEB 1984.

11 April 1850

Dear Friends, brothers and sisters:

In the end, it has taken a half year for the trip from the time we left Strausney until our arrival. You have accurately heard how long we had to wait in Hamburg for a ship and that on 21 December before the Christmas holiday we were finally able to sail. Our ship "ALEXANDER" was pretty and well built, and her captain skilled as a sailor and very friendly and good to us. Our quarters on the upper deck were adequate and habitable; our fellow travelers between the lower decks, however, were in bad conditions.

The ship, with space for 150 passengers, was half full from the start of the voyage. We spent our Christmas holidays on a calm ocean, though there was a great storm on Ash Wednesday. A strong wind started on Tuesday and this developed large waves and swells on Wednesday; Thursday and Friday it stormed without stopping and we did not see the sun in the daytime nor the stars at night - and even the captain was concerned. The conditions were scary and it was noticed how the mood of the people changed as they prepared to withstand the large swells and stormy winds. My greatest concern in all this rough weather was for the women and children who, in their sickness, could not hold themselves in their bunks and were afraid of being thrown out of their beds.

I and my family were not bad sick and other passengers did not understand how I could help my close friends and serve them in their sickness. I spent much time on deck holding to the railing and spent hours looking about and wondering about life during the storm. What I saw and felt then, I cannot describe in writing to anyone who has not experienced this situation. The ocean calmed down Sunday at 4:30 and after a refreshing nap, we were happy to learn we were between England and France. The sun came out and on one side, we saw the cliffs of England and on the other side the blue waters toward France.

On 31 December 1849, we stopped at the English port of Portsmouth so the ship could take on more passengers who awaited us here. On New Year's, I held services and gave thanks to the Lord for having protected us during the storm in which, I later learned, two ships (English and American) were shipwrecked. Calmness came after the winds and the children played happily on deck where we warmed ourselves in the sun. While our ship was at the dock, I looked around to see what was in the town and saw mainly the English ships which were as large as our homes and castles, and I wondered how the ocean can "push" them around.

Sunday after the New Year, we were furbished with fresh water and meat and sailed on. Our deck was normal and a happy one until we encountered the large waves and swells of the ocean; then most became seasick except the sailors; they had to vomit and their heads began to hurt so that they could hardly stay on their feet - but this sickness is not lasting or dangerous. Our food was not tasteful, perhaps because of the seasickness, and consisted of: dried peas three times a week, beans one day, rice once and once or twice we had rolls; then pork twice per week and salted beef on other days. In the morning we had black coffee and green tea at night with cookies made from wheat flour and without yeast; baked kolache twice a week but so hard that they were suitable only for good teeth, although quite tasteful with butter brushed on. At the end, we were served kraut and potatoes in lieu of the dried peas and rice - and this tasted better. In addition, one received a half pound of butter, a half pound of sugar, and on Sunday a bottle of wine! Then it began to get warmer.

On 16 January 1850, there came a warm rain as would come to you on St. Johns.

On 17 January 1850, the sun came out at 6:45 and it was so bright and clear that one wondered - because never does the sun shine this brightly in Europe. Every day I waited for the sunrise on deck just so I could get a view of this beautiful sun. We had warm temperatures of 20 - 24 degrees Celsius.

On 25 January 1850, we arrived at the sign of the Crab and found hot temperatures of 20 - 24 deg. C. Here I saw, for the first time, the aurora borealis. The moon and the stars have an unusual appearance here and the nights are so different that a person stands for long hours and contemplates.

26 January 1850: We reached the half way mark on our road to America! Our route now takes us more northerly and then we will go to the south. The winds started to blow and in 24 hours we traveled forty to fifty miles of our journey; the mornings and nights were pretty - but the noon is sultry. Whales are seen daily and they come even to the ship and think nothing about the three guns that were fired into their midst. They are a strange animal and spray water through their noses which looks very pretty. There are other smaller fish, especially porpoises (dolphins) which are so numerous that we hardly noticed them. European birds have long left us so we see only the fish.

6 February 1850: The ocean was covered with a green moss (Saragasso Sea) and we pulled some of it aboard the ship. We saw it had white bulbs, something smaller than garlic or onions, and these are salty.

8 February 1850: We saw the Island of Haiti for the first land! Ach, even I cannot write of our gladness because for a long time we saw only the ocean and the heavens, and here we again see beautiful blue mountains and forests.

9 February, Saturday: The hog was killed and we picked our way further by the Islands of Haiti and Cuba - and for the occasion, on Sunday, we ate the whole hog! Tuesday, the ship was aimed toward the north so that the Island of Cuba was left to the side. American birds began to fly around the ship. We suffered from the heat now and the captain let us prepare for a bath which enlivened myself and others.

23 February 1850: We saw America but it was so foggy that we had to stop.

27 February 1850: Wednesday at 6:00 in the night, we arrived offshore at Galveston and anchored close to the town.

1 March 1850: On Friday, our Captain went ashore.

2 March 1850: At 3:00 in the afternoon, we left our ship "ALEXANDER" and rode a small American tug into Galveston where, at 6:00 in the night, we stepped for the first time on American land (soil). We lodged at a small German hotel "At the Stars".

4 March 1850: On Tuesday, I found a place to stay in another home because in the hotel we were required to pay one-half dollar per day per person (about one "zlaty" silver). So we lived on the boat from 20 January 1849 until 2 March 1850 and from the 6th of January to the 8th of February, we saw nothing other than the heavens and the ocean!

Galveston, a town in Texas, counts about a 5000 population and all homes, save the church and the Bureau (Federal Building) are built of wood and covered with oil paint for in such a warm climate other types of dwellings are not needed.

On our arrival, the potatoes were just in bloom and the gardens had English peas. The trees were going into bloom and leaf: carrots, lettuce, turnips and other kitchen vegetables were fresh for pulling. Before each home, there were roses planted which bloomed very beautifully. Other trees, such as oleander, orange and lemon, were in bloom and could be smelled everywhere.

However, we who had intended to settle in Galveston did not like conditions here. There were very many mosquitoes and the children were getting sores like smallpox and became sick.

12 March 1850: We left on a steamboat from Galveston for the Brazos River and changed to another steamboat at Quintana at the mouth of the Brazos. We traveled upstream on the Brazos. This was a very exciting trip as there were large trees overhanging the banks. Plantations were located at intervals where we saw negros working with cotton and sugar cane, all of which grew profusely. There is a large concentration of these unlucky negros - that is, "slaves" - in Galveston, perhaps as many as 1000 head.

One young strong and healthy slave costs 800 - 1000 dollars per head, a woman slave 500 - 800 dollars, boy from eight to ten years, 100 - 200 dollars; because everybody who is able wishes to buy a slave for work. But so you, even though you are Christians, feel that keeping a human in bondage is not proper, I wish to tell you that these negros live in a better way than the poor people in Cechy and Moravia. They receive coffee twice a day, meat and bread three times daily, with good milk, as much as they wish, because each plantation has more than 1000 head of livestock. They are occupied with working in the fields, grazing the livestock, and cleaning and butchering same. I saw those slaves playing with the "dollar" same as your boys play with a button.

16 March 1850: Saturday afternoon we arrived at San Felipe; a prominent town destroyed so thoroughly during the war with Mexico that only about fifteen homes remain. Here we stayed with a German merchant who hosted us until the 19th of March. On 17 March, we visited the American rural countryside for the first time and saw pretty tall grass. Cattle freely grazed on it and the children picked the beautiful flowers, some

of which in your country are grown in clay flower pots! I and my daughter Julia and the maid Justina, sat down on the grass and sang "Ja ve vaem mem cineni jen k bohu mam sve zreni" (I in all my deeds have only respect for God), and we thought of you that just now you are returning from the afternoon church services. Here it is 9:45 before noon, and at your place it would be 3:30 in the afternoon since the sun is six and a quarter hours later here.

Tuesday on the day of St. Josef, we loaded our baggage on a wagon and two oxen carried it to our intended place of living, where we happily arrived that same day before night. Here we stayed with a Merchant and farmer named Boulton, son of a pastor from Hamburg for whom we had two letters from Europe. We found our stay friendly. Here in his garden, we planted 21 trees which we brought from Europe; also some seed was sown and we planted several rows of potatoes. The surroundings are very beautiful, the soil is black mixed with sand and three fruitful layers deep.

Not far from Mr. Boulton lives a buyer, also from Europe who lives an ugly life. He cheats and wrongly treats his fellow citizens and from this he hopes to become rich.

Tuesday after Palm Sunday, a terrible storm came up and lightning hit the house of the buyer. He had many hundreds of dollars of goods on display and it all burned. No one came to put the fire out because he has had too many quarrels and suits and there were no volunteers. There was no loss to the community and he came to the end of his name. He then moved to Galveston so that he would not have to return to working in the field.

At that same time, the evangelical group met in the community center near Cat Springs, about a mile by the road from Mr. Boulton where it is planned to build a school building. On Saturday before Palm Sunday, I took off for this center so that I could arrange and discuss various things; however it was not possible to do this because it had already been arranged that I was to hold church services at Mr. Boultons on Good Friday. An Evangelical missionary from South Carolina came to this gathering. He was young, healthy and a good speaker, and had already gathered people together to whom he preached. Arrangements were made with him that Easter services would be celebrated at Cat Springs and the Lord's Supper held: and we both left in agreement. On that day (Easter) a larger crowd of people from all sides then gathered, which I had expected, and the large room at Mr. Amsler could not contain all of us - the greater number had to stand by the windows and the doors.

At the conclusion of this service, I was voted unanimously to serve as their spiritual pastor and a yearly salary of one hundred dollars was assured me - each voted on this of their own free will and more than one openly agreed to give eight dollars per year. I accepted this assignment and in order to be better able to serve my listeners, I bought myself a small house near Cat Springs, which has one setting room, two closets and a small sleeping room. There is a small three-quarter acre garden near the house and a fifteen acre field which is not plowed.

On the 5th of April, our neighbors came for us with two wagons and we somehow managed to get settled. Today in the afternoon, April 7,1850, it is planned that we will hold another church service under the same shelter on 17 April unless the listeners decide otherwise. We now have the most beautiful weather and winds; the afternoons are warm but the nights are cool and fine when the fireflies come out and swarm about. The redbirds, here called "Cardinals", sing in the woods and the trees around the house, their song being similar to the nightingale in Europe.

The land here west of San Felipe and five miles from the Brazos River, is not sultry and humid since the winds blow steadily, and there is no fever which exists in some lowlands. There is none of the prevalent human ailments, mainly of the chest, and whoever would come here with a lung ailment will get well quickly. I know two neighbors who, as they told me, with their damaged lungs would already have been laid long ago in their cold bed, whereas here they got completely well. In the lowlands (bottomland) we have very productive lands, so rich that they never need to be fertilized; however, it is unhealthy to live there and for this reason, the colony and settlements is found on the highlands where there is healthy weather. The bottom land fields of the rich planters and settlers is worked by negros, but the highlands grow Turkish wheat (corn) eight to ten feet high. Rye and wheat are not yet planted here as first, there is no mill to grind the grain, and second, it has not been proven to be successfully grown and harvested. Corn, however, grows well in the small valleys and is more productive. So the settlers bake bread made from corn. The corn is ground daily on small hand mills similar to those one has for coffee. The larger corn grain particles are fed to the chickens which everybody here has large flocks of, sometimes in two coops. The small corn flour is prepared with milk and eggs and baked on an iron plate above the coals, although it is still not as good as bread from buckwheat baked in an oven.

Others in the neighboring settlements are able to get enough wheat flour but again there is no bakery or yeast shop, not even a beer brewery. According to a late word, the rumor is out that members of the settlement are planning an Evangelical Church and mill!

Each family has a fenced field here but the remaining land is open and basically used for grazing cattle and horses, however many a person wants; there are hogs beyond count because if you ask someone how many he has, he cannot tell you.

Now I would like to tell you something about our neighbors, but first about the closest.

Ondrej Laass from between Berlin and Magdeburg, lived a long time in Prussia where he saved enough that four years ago he was able and emigrated to America through Bremen. He came alone, had nothing except his healthy body, and had to go to work for others. Now he is well off, has two hundred acres of land, fifty head of cattle, eleven horses and so many hogs that he doesn't even know how many; and to add to that, he has five sons old enough to work and he himself is a strong and diligent worker.

Our other neighbor was a boatman, unloading from the ships in Galveston. Four years ago, he bought land here and now has his own livestock and a healthy sum of cash. Laass, however, has 600 dollars and is thinking of buying a negro for his work.

The third is Haljn who has been here six years and counts among the better-off: he has 100 head of cattle and twenty horses.

However, of all the oldest and first settlers, is surely Mr. Amsler, born a Swiss. He came here more than fifteen years ago, but brought nothing but his health and working hands; and now he has a pretty home, hotel and a store, 1500 acres of land besides two other houses, 300 head of cattle and 100 horses.

From this, it is possible to see that an industrious and working man can soon bring into himself some wealth. However, it is to be noted that "here without work, there are no kolache!" and anyone who is not industrious will soon return to Europe.

I have already brought two cows with calves for ten dollars and soon will be able to buy a horse so that I may be able to ride in our settlement, or perhaps to San Felipe, some five miles. I already have eighteen hens and a neighbor has promised me some hogs. I will work and fence four acres of field for the fall and will plant cotton because it brings the most. I hope, if God gives me good health, to have more in a few years - but the start is always hard.

Beggars and robbers are not found here and people do not close their doors nor do they have concern for their fields. On our journey, we slept some distance from our wagons and nothing happened to us. In short, no one is concerned about stealing what belongs to others. My wife lost her satchel and in it she had some toiletries and some money. But see, in eight days, our neighbor brought it to us and said it was given to him by a stranger who said it belongs in our settlement!

There are not many people in Texas which is a land as large as Germany and Prussia put together. Texas today has 200,000 inhabitants which is the same as Breslau alone. There are only a few women who are able to come to Texas from Europe and hence these are in great demand. Our maid, Justina, already could have gotten married three times to proper and occupied youths, but she has not yet decided on anyone. Besides that, she has to serve at our home for a time in exchange for the boat fare we paid for her. That will not last long and she will soon leave us and go to her own home and household on a beautiful saddled horse, and if she is fortunate, her groom will bring her the beautiful saddled horse as a gift.

There is here an assortment of various trees such as oaks, maple, nut and so forth. There are forests five miles to the north with cedars and cypresses from which we are able to get boards (lumber). The trees in the forests grow wild, large and tall - from the ground up to the heavens.

You will be able to visualize how it actually all looks from all this I have said, as I have told you the whole clear truth. Whoever wishes to say good by to Europe should emigrate through Bremen to America because the ocean voyage from there is better arranged and cheaper than from Hamburg.

I wish to add that here we have many grouse (Prairie Chickens) and deer. Now, they are shooting turkeys and deer and Mr. Boltin killed a grouse which I saw with my own eyes that weighed twenty pounds. The quail and cranes here are smaller than in Europe but they swarm so no one hardly notices, though they don't stand to be shot. I have not yet had time to go on a hunt. Bees are kept at houses and can be found everywhere in the hollow trees; they swarm from spring to fall - but go into their hives or holes because with the snow and frost, they cannot live. The bees are "robbed" twice, in May and September.

I will repeat once again that emigrants should start on their journey in the fall because in the summer it is dangerous and unhealthy. The best is to organize in groups with families.

You all be good - God be with you!

Early Marriages in Austin County
(from court house records)
Probable Residents of Mill Creek Forks Area

Date	Husband	Wife
20 Apr 1826	Ignatius Burns	Sara Kuykendall
13 Nov 1828	Thomas Bell	Abigail Grimes
21 Oct 1829	Robert Ray	Margarette Grimes
5 Aug 1830	Charles Benton	Nancy Grimes
13 July 1835	Wm. J. Eaton	Amanda Bostic
4 Sept 1837	Renke Stolkey	Margaret Burns
7 Nov 1837	Robt. Kuykendall	Sectra Shannon
29 July 1838	Adam Kuykendall	Susan Grimes
8 Oct 1838	George Grimes	Tracy Yerkins
8 Oct 1838	Gibson Kuykendall	Martha Kuykendall
19 Apr 1840	Mathew Kuykendall	Mary H. Gentry
27 Jan 1841	George W. Grimes	Mrs. Martha Williams
9 Dec 1841	Alexander Glenn	Sarah P. Shelburne
24 Feb 1842	Andrew J. Bell	Calpernia H. Shelburne
7 Apr 1842	Elias Elliott	Francis Ward
1 Oct 1842	Wm. Norcross	Susan Kuykendall
13 June 1844	William G. Grimes	Mary Riggs
7 Nov 1844	Nathan French	Margaret A. Terry
23 Jan 1845	Samuel A. Shelburn	Juline A. Bell
29 Dec 1845	William L. Shelburn	Jane A. Terry
5 Sept 1846	Benjamin S. Harrison	Lucinda Grimes
1 Dec 1846	Solomon Ward	Manda Sullivan
2 Aug 1847	Hillyard Terry	Mary J. Radford
16 Aug 1847	Charles E. Hilburn	Virginia A. Shelburn
26 Apr 1849	J. W. Kuykendall	Elizabeth Duff
6 Sept 1849	William L. Shelburn	Mary C. Terry
28 Nov 1849	Samuel J. Grimes	Caroline Kahan
12 Dec 1849	Franklin Elliot	Harret Terry
31 Dec 1849	W.R.A. Terry	Louna Londa Elliott
24 Dec 1850	Jesse Ward	Elitha Ann Elliott
22 Mar 1851	William Wells	Lydia Norcross
19 Oct 1855	William M. Sherril	Elisabeth Norcross
8 Feb 1858	David D. Nelson	Mrs. Sarah E. Slaughter
9 Aug 1859	J.H. Campbell	Susan Elliott
22 Mar 1861	Charles N. Quillen	Mary Ann Elliott
28 Feb 1862	R.P. White	Mrs. Susan A. Elliott
19 Mar 1873	G.L. Humble	Catherine Norcross

1850 United States Census

The following are selected entries from the Austin County, Texas, 1850 census. The county was not subdivided in this census, so all entries are under the single place heading "Austin County". Thus, it is impossible to identify all residents in the lower forks of Mill Creek. These names were selected from other indications of their residence or association with settlement in the area.

Name	Age	Occupation	Property	Born
Samuel Shelborn	57	farmer	$600R	VA
Nancy	45			TN
Henry	21			
Samuel	19			
Mary	16			
Wm. Ward	22			
John	13			
Sarah Nelson	20			IN
Bluford Nelson	2			AL
Samuel Shelborn	33	farmer	$800R	TN
Adeline	28			AL
James	5			
?	3			
Sarah	1			
Wm. Shelborn	27	farmer	$600R	TN
Mary	17			AL
Wm.	4			TX
Sarah	2/12			TX
J.P Shelborn	59	farmer		VA
Nancy	53			VA
Henry	24			TN
Lu ?	16			AL
Andrew	14			AL
June Durkin?	80			VA
Mariah Shelborn	16			TX
GC	22			TN
G	28			SC
John Ward	30	farmer	$1212R	NC
Marthe	22			TN

Jasper	2			TX
?	3/12			TX
James S. Bethany	26	farmer	$1000R	AL
Adeline	24			AL
Mary	5			AL
Thomas	3			AL
James	3/12			TX
Thomas Bethany	72	farmer		SC
Rebecca	55			SC
A (female)	47			SC
M. Terry	50	farmer	$1994	SC
Mary	52			SC
William	24			AL
Amanda	15			MS
Martha	12			MS
H. Eliot	23	laborer		NC
Harriot Eliot	18			AL
William	1/12			TX
Elias Elliot	32	farmer	$1000	NC
Frances	26			NC
? (m)	8			TX
David Ward	18	laborer		NC
Wm. Eliot	23	farmer		NC
Samuel Eliot	24	schoolteacher		NC
Joshua Ward	22	farmer		NC
A.M. Logan	40	farmer	$410	TN
Elizabeth	25			AL
John H. Lee	35	farmer	$500	TN
Samuel Eliot	40	carpenter	$1700	TN
Nancy	39			KY
James	18			TX
Elizabeth	16			TX
Frances	11			TX
Susan	9			TX
George	8			TX
Samuel	6			TX
Mary	4			TX

William	2			TX
Margaret	1			TX
Milton? Eliot	20	laborer		TN
Alfred Minton	47	farmer	$1120	SC
Jane	34			TN
Robert	17			AL
Samuel	9			TX
?	6			TX
Virginia	3			TX
John Atkinson	56	farmer	$4693	NC
Mariah	49			SC
John	25	wagoneer	$75	AL
Alexander	22		$70	AL
Catherine	23			AL
Nancy	19			AL
Martha	18			AL
Jane	13			TX
Solomon	10			TX
Alex Jones	21	wagoneer		TN
Thomas Nichols	22	farmer		TX
Mary	18			Holland
James Bailey	28	schoolteacher		LA
Wm. Northcross	35	farmer	$200	NY
Eleonore	43		$100	NY
Mary	20			IN
Liddie	16			OH
Ann	14			IN
Eliza	12			IN
Catherine	8			TX
John	5			TX
George French	38	blacksmith		SC
G. W. Grimes	29			KY
Martha	29			AR
Elizabeth	15			
Mary				
Fredrick				

R. C. Burns	48 M	farmer	NC
Achsah Burns	37 F		NC
Thomas	16 M		NC
Sarah	15 F		AL
Nacissa (Narcissa)	12 F		AL
Francis (Frances?)	11 F		AL
Felix	9 M		MS
Junis (John)	8 M		TX
Nancy	6 F		TX
Joanah (Joan D'Arch)	5 F		TX
Tobias (Napolean)	3 M		TX
Mary Burns	24 F		NC
John	3 M		TX

1850 United States Census - Austin County, Texas
Slave Schedules

Owner	No.	Age	Sex	Race
Solomon Ward	1	18	M	B
	1	14	F	B
	1	6	F	M
J. P. Shelborne	1	36	F	B
	1	36	M	B
	1	28	F	B
	1	21	M	B
	1	19	F	B
	1	16	M	B
	1	14	F	B
	1	10	M	B
	1	8	M	B
	1	6	M	B
	1	5	F	B
	1	3	M	B
	1	2	F	B
	1	1/12	F	B
Rufus Campbell	5			
Samuel Shelborne	1	17	M	B
	1	1	M	B

William Shelborne	1	9	M	B
E. C. Williamson	1	8	F	B
A. Minton	1	18	F	B
	1	17	M	B
	1	11	F	B
John Ward	1	10	F	B
	1	24	M	B
Thomas Bethany	1	60	F	B
	3	40	F	B
	1	32	F	B
	3	30	M	B
	1	28	F	B
	2	20	F	B
	2	20	M	B
	2	18	F	B
	1	17	F	B
	2	16	M	B
	1	14	F	B
	1	13	F	B
	1	12	F	B
	4	10	M	B
	1	10	F	B
	2	8	M	B
	2	6	F	B
	3	6	M	B
	2	4	M	B
	1	3	F	B
	2	2	M	B
	1	2	F	B
	1	1	M	B
	1	2/12	F	B
M. Terry	1	40	M	B
	1	40	F	B
	1	33	M	B
	1	20	M	B
	1	20	M	B
	1	18	M	B

	1	18	F	B
	1	16	M	B
Wm. Norcross	1	38	M	B
James Daughtry	1	42	M	B
	1	36	M	B
	1	36	F	B
	1	17	M	B
	1	16	F	B
	1	12	M	B
	1	10	M	B
	1	9	M	B
	2	6	F	B
Samuel Elliot	1	17	F	B

1860 United States Census

The following is a complete listing of the Forkston entries (head of household only, with number listed in family group) from the 1860 census microfilms. It appears that some of the census is missing; the first page of the entries begin with a listing of children of the Willis family, and no head of household. The next entry is number 429, which implies that entry numbers 1 - 428 are missing. However, the 1900 Census only listed 257 family groups in the "Nelsonville" precinct, so the land area defined by the Census precincts must have changed. The German names are very hard to read and most are spelled as the English phonetic equivalent.

Entry	Name	Age	No.	Occupation	Born
429	W. A. Thompson	26	3	farmer	AL
430	Thomas H. Bradbury	26	2	"	NY
431	Aaron M. Logan	50	3	"	TN
432	I. H. Campbell	30	2	carpenter	NC
433	John Manley	42	7	farmer	NC
434	E. C. Williamson	26	6	?	GA
435	Elias Elliott	44	5	farmer	NC
436	Mary Howard	49	10	"	TN
437	B. Creekmore	40	7	"	VA
438	Edward Daughtry	34	4	"	TX
439	Hermon Hebron ?	31	7	"	Germany
440	Peter James	45	8	"	SC
441	Charles Beges ?	46	2	"	Germany
442	F. W. Miller	43	7	"	"
443	Henry Peters	35	5	"	"
444	R. Haetge	74	9	"	"
	Henry Wilke	65		schoolteacher	"
445	B. F. Schmitt	56	3	farmer	"
446	Wm. Fortran	23	1	farmer	TX
447	T. D. Ledbetter	27	1	"	TN
448	Malcolm Majar	66	3	"	Scotland
449	Wm. Hewett	52	1	"	NC
450	Charles Fox	41	7	"	Germany
451	H. John	45	7	"	"
452	G. Frickey ?	39	8	"	"
453	Charles Hoff	54	9	shoemaker	"
454	Frederick Sedaw ?	33	5	farmer	"
455	I. Lass ?	39	6	"	Swiss
456	? Miller	34	2	"	"
457	John M. McClann	32	4	"	NC

458	D. H. Shillig	50	5	"	Germany
459	Edward Stiefs ?	28	5	"	Swiss
460	John Stiefs ?	30	2	"	"
461	F. Hughfield	24	2	"	Germany
462	A. Clatt	48	6	"	"
463	James Vogelsang ?	56	7	"	"
464	W. O. Spainks ?	35	4	blacksmith	"
465	Theodore Horac ?	32	6	merchant	"
466	Casper Vitern ?	33	2	farmer	"
467	Wm. Colbern ?	40	2	"	"
468	Virgil ? dollar	62	2	"	"
469	Christian Shafner ?	32	4	laborer	"
470	W. R. Whittington	33	8	farmer	GA
471	Irene Telf ?	46	4	seamstress	GA
472	Otto Betican ?	28	3	farmer	Germany
473	Henry Aben	35	4	"	"
474	I. C. Whittington	37	6	"	SC
475	S. A. Shelborn	43	10	"	TN
476	S. P. Shelborn	70	1	"	VA
477	S. H. Shelborn	35	1	"	TN
478	A. B. Shelborn	25	3	"	AL
479	M. B. Hairston	21	2	"	GA
480	G. G. McGregor	35	2	"	NC
481	August Becker	26	3	"	GA
482	H. Eldridge	54	4	"	NH
483	Henry Smith	25	4	"	KY
484	H. H. Peebles	28	3	"	FL
485	W. Peebles	27	1	"	FL
486	S. V. Evans	46	3	"	VA
487	Henry A. Ward	26	2	"	TN
488	I. C. Brooks	34	7	"	GA
489	James Redford	65	4	"	VA
490	? Cleves ?	28	5	"	LA
491	F. B. Shoemaker	27	4	wagoneer	SC
492	Henry Shelborn	31	3	farmer	AL
493	S. H. Wasserman ?	38	4	"	Germany
494	Wm. F. Ward	32	6	"	TN
495	A. Brownstein ?	54	7	"	Germany
496	S. P. Shelborn	54	7	"	VA
497	S. P. Shelborn	22	2	"	AL
498	E. W. Morris	38	6	"	AL
499	Fred ?	27	2	"	Germany
500	Otto Cabbunge ?	28	5	"	"

501	James Baron	30	6	"	TX
502	John Osdner ?	41	6	"	Germany
503	L. A. Cummings	32	6	"	TX
504	J. A. Thompson	53	2	"	KY
505	Harmon Meigs	38	6	"	Germany
506	Sarah Whittington	56	2	"	SC
507	F. G. Telf ?	28	4	"	GA
508	Wm. Barnhill	40	10	"	GA
	S. P. Ladland	22		teacher AL	
509	G. W. Shields	45	3	farmer	AL
510	N. Davis	52	6	farmer	NC
511	J. M. Jackson	27	2	overseer	NC
512	Aschabel Whitby	50	6	farmer	TN
513	Tepe ? Ward	37	6	"	NC
514	Theo. Flake	60	6	"	SC
515	George Ball	59	2	"	SC
516	Wm. Lassinbury ?	35	2	"	Germany
517	William Shelborn	36	8	"	LA
518	J. W. Bethany	36	9	"	AL
519	John Ward	40	4	"	NC
520	Thos. Bethany	83	2	"	SC
521	M. Terry	60	3	"	SC
522	W. Terry	34	7	"	AL
523	H. Terry	35	7	"	AL
524	John Meridith ?	28	2	"	GA
525	I. Bonner	56	5	"	GA
526	Wm. P. Elliott	30	5	"	NC
527	I. H. Minton	43	5	"	TN
528	R. Minton	27	1	"	AL
529	? I. Bell	43	6	"	AL
530	R. T. Paine	49	1	"	NC
	J. N. Daniel	29	2	"	GA

The following are selected entries from the 1860 census of Austin County, Texas. They were chosen as having some connection to lower Mill Creek forks area.

Name	Age	Occupation	Property	Born
Industry:				
R. G. Burns	54	farmer		VA
A wife (Achsah)				NC
Phillip (Felix)	18			MS
John	17			TX
Daniel	12			TX
Napoleon	10			TX
Mary F	30	teacher		NC
M. F.	20			AL
Nancy	15			TX
Forkston (Pecan Grove Precinct):				
Elias Elliot	44	farmer	$4800R,$5000P	NC
Frances	38			NC
Y.L.	17			TX
M.A.	15			TX
L.B.	4			TX
B. Creekmore	40	farmer	$1200R, $300P	VA
Eleanor	33			IN
Albert	11			
Dudley	9			
R.J.	7			
?	5			
Mary F.	2			
L. A. Shelborn	43	farmer	$4000R, $5000P	TN
Adale	35			TN
JA 14, IA 12, A 11, J 9, N 7, WB 6, C 4, SA 1				TX
S. P. Shelborn	70		$10,800R, $16,800PVA	
I. H. Shelborn	35		$5000	TN
A.B. Shelborn	25		$1,500R, $4,000P	AL
Em wife	22			TX
CC	2			TX
G.C. McGregor	35	farmer $176,000, $1800		NC
Pattie	21			TX

Henry Shelborn	31	farmer	$1200, $1000	AL
L.P. Shelborn	65	farmer	$4000, $1800	VA
EA (child)	12			AL
J.P. Shelborn	22			AL
wife				
L.A. Thompson (f)	53			KY
M.I. (f)	12			MO
William Shelborn	36			LA
Nancy	26			SC
Children	10,8,6,4,3,1,			TX
J. W. Bethany	36	farmer	$2000, $2000	AL
wife	35			AL
child (f)	15			AL
children	13,10,7,5,3,3			TX
John Ward	40	farmer	$1500,$5600	NC
wife	31			TN
children	12,8			TX
Thos. Bethany	83	farmer	$17,800	SC
R (wife)	68			SC
M. Terry	60	farmer	$8000, $15000	SC
Nancy	62			SC
I Bonner	31	laborer	$10000	AL
I. Bonner	56	farmer	$5000, $22000	GA
Nancy	47			AL
W.L. Bonner	24	overseer		AL
B.W. Bonner	31	overseer		AL
Wm. P Eliot	30	farmer	$320, $300	NC
Sarah	29			AL
children	6,5,1			

1860 United States Census
Slave Inhabitants - Austin County, Texas

Owner	Age	Sex	Age	Sex
<u>Bellville:</u>				
John Atkinson	33	M	19	M
W. L. Shelborne	20	F	1	F
Jesse Ward	25	M		
Wm. Shelborne	25	F	20	M
	18	M	17	F
	3	M	2	F
	1	F		
John Ward	30	M	17	F
Thomas Bethany	70	F	45	F
	40	M	31	F
	28	F	26	M
	18	M	15	M
	12	F	11	F
	7	M	5	M
	5	F	1	F
	1	M	1	F
A. M. Logan	23	M	20	F
	13	M		
M. Terry	50	M	50	F
	24	M	15	M
	20	F	11	M
	7	M	5	F
	2	F	1	F
J. M. L. Bonner	55	M	30	F
	20	M	10	F
	9	F	5	M
	1	M	1	F

	1	M		
J. W. Bethany	53	M	39	M
	38	M	29	M
	25	M	25	F
	25	F	25	F
	18	M	9	F
	7	M	5	M
	1	F	1	F
George W. Foster	60	M	60	F
	30	M	28	F
	25	F	24	M
	24	F	15	M
	12	F	10	F
	8	F	4	M
	1	M	1	F
	1/12	M		
B. F. Foster	50	M	35	F
	30	F	25	F
	25	M	23	M
	18	M	15	F
	12	M	9	F
	8	F	5	M

<u>Hempstead:</u>

D. D. Nelson	19	F		

<u>Pecan Grove:</u>

S. A. Shelborne	25	F	17	F
	2	M		
John P. Shelborne	48	M	47	F
	40	F	40	M
	28	M	27	F
	20	M	15	F
	14	M	14	F

	12	F	8	F
	6	M	4	M
	1	F		
A. B. Shelborne	23	F	21	M
	5	F		
J. H. Shelborne	29	F	18	M
	16	F	1	F
S. P. Shelborne	17	F	1	F
A. B. Houston	40	M	15	F
	8	F		
G. R. McGregor	27	M		
Wm. Terry	7			
J. T. Terry	2			
J. N. Daniel	45	M	40	M
	35	M	35	F
	26	M	26	M
	22	M	12	M
	5	F		
E. M. Bethany	40	F	35	F
	23	F	17	M
	16	F	15	F
	12	F	8	F
	6	M	4	M
	2	F	1	F
D. F. Willis	15	F	1	F
Wm. A. Thompson	13	M	2	M
John Manley	25	M	18	F
	15	F	16	M
	12	F	9	F
	1	M		

Elias Elliot	15	M	15	M
Mary Howard	35	F	10	M
	8	M	8	M
Edward Daughtry	45	M	35	M
	34	F	22	F
	21	M	9	F
	5	F	5	M
	1	F		
Malcolm Magor	20			
Wm. Hewitt	12			

Pine Grove:

Jordan Bonner	40	F	30	M
	26	F	20	F
	20	M	18	F
	18	M	17	F
	15	F	15	F
	14	M	16	M
	13	F	5	M
	3	F		
I. H. Minton	30	F	28	F
	10	M	9	M
	6	F	4	F
	2	M	1	M
	1	F		

Cat Springs:

James Daughtry	40	M	30	F
	17	M	8	F
	5	M		

1870 United States Census

The residents between the forks of Mill Creek were counted in the 1870 census in the "Industry" district. There were 805 households listed in this grouping. The following entries were selected as probable residents in the lower forks of Mill Creek.

Industry:

Name	Age	Race	Occupation	Assets Real, Personal	Born
Wm. Elliott	25	B	farm labor		Dis. Col.
Adelea	24	B			TX
James	5				TX
Charles	25		farm labor		DC
E	19				MS
Elizabeth	2				TX
James Daughtry	47		farmer	$500, $500	TX
Isabella	38				AL
George Foster	36		doctor	$4000,$1500	IL
Betty	22				AL
Frank ?	11				TX
Charles	1				TX
Jane Minton	54		farmer	$4000, $2500	TN
Robert	38				AL
Virginia	20				TX
Homer Bradbury	33		farmer	$600, $600	NY
Margaret	31				NC
Wm.	18				TX
John	8				TX
Sally	6				TX
(f)	4				TX
(f)	2				TX
Breamby, ?	46	B		$400 P	NC
Frances	36	B			AL
	9,8,5,5,2				TX
Elias Elliott	52		farmer	$6000, $1500	NC
Frances	47				NC
Frances	28				TX

Solomon	14				TX
John Ward	51	W	farmer	$3500, $500	NC
wife	42				TN
Solomon	18				
Martha	9				
Jack					
David Ward	38				
Jesse Ward	44 and family				NC
Ruffin Ward	45 and family				NC
David Bonner	30	B	farmer	$1000, $500	GA
Mary	29	B			TX
David	11				TX
Phillis	7				TX
Alexander	2				TX
David Nelson	46	W	farmer	$2500, $500	GA
Sarah	36				AL
Sarah	11				TX
Becky	5				TX
Georgia	1				TX
Alexander Bonner	29	W	farm labor		AL
Rachel	26				AL
Amanda	8				TX
Joseph	3				TX
Robert Bonner	45	W	farm labor		AL
James Bethany	46		farmer	$16000, $4000	AL
Mary	45				AL
Wm.	17				TX
Lucinda	15				TX
Isabella	13				TX
Serana	13				TX
Ella	11				TX
Cal ?(f)	5				TX
Jenny	6/12				TX
Dick Bonner	4	W	living with McKee, Manley		TX
Anna	20				

John	14				
Georgia	9				
Amanda	5				
John Schiller	55				Austria
Rosalie	48				Austria
John	22				Austria
Amalia	15				TX
Theresa	14				TX
Frances	12				TX
Samuel, Carl, Joseph, Johanna					TX
Jacob Bonner	25	B			AL
Susky	27				AL
Rachel	11				TX
R. Burns	68	W	farmer		NC
Agnes(Achsah)	58				NC
Felix	29				
John	27				
Nancy	25				
A (Napolean)	22				
Mary	41				
Travis Burns	10	B			TX
Eggie Burns	25	Bf	domestic servant		VA
Wm.	3	mulatto			TX
David Bonner	56	B	farm labor		AL
wife	51				AL
Mary	15				TX
children	11,11				TX
Allen	7				TX
Ellen	4				TX
Richard Ward	45	B			AL
wife	50				MI
child	20				LA
David	18				LA
Andrew	16				LA
James	13				LA
Phillip	2				TX
Wm. Norcross	60	W	farmer	$6000,$500	NJ

Samuel	10				TX
Margaret Stevens	30				AL
Martha	11				
George Norcross	26		farm labor		TX
Mary	27				TX
John	1				
John Shelborn	70	W	farmer	$5000,$1000	VA
Wm. Shelborn	47			$12000, $6000	TN
Mary	38				
Nancy	16				TX
John	14				TX
Isabella	12				TX
Jefferson	9				TX
Issac	6				TX
Homer	4				TX
Jackson	2				TX
Henry Daughtry	25	B	farm labor		AL
Clarcy	28				AL
Bethany (?)	51	B	farm labor		AL
Jane	39				NC
M.	17				TX
Maxwell	11				TX
Travis	8				TX
Nelson Shelborn	29	B	farm labor		TX
Angelina	25				TX
Martha	6				TX
Banks	4				TX
E	3				TX
James Bethany	20			$3000, $4000	TX
David Knolle	27	B	farms (rents)		AL
Wm. Bethany	24	B	farms (rents)		TX
John Kraulik	35		farmer	$1500, $350	Austria
Franziska	30				
Wm.	2				

Marie	1/2				
Thomas Shelborn	23	B	farmer (rents)$250		TX
George Shelborn	56	B	farmer (rents) $500		TX
Allen Bethany	26	B			AL
S.C. McGregor	45		Doctor, farmer, medic		NC
John Mikeska	60		farmer	$2000,$600	Austria
Rosina	55				"
Josef	23				"
Rosina	28				"
Franz	16				"
Franziska	11				"
John Mikeska	32		farmer	$120,$600	
Johanna	36				
Franz Matshak	19		farm labor		
Joseph Susen	58			$3000,$500	
Anna	52				
John	16				
Rosine	12				
John Schiller	55				Austria
Rosalie	48				"
John	22				"
Annalie	15				TX
Theresia	14				TX
Franziska	12				TX
Louise	11				TX
Johanna	4				TX
Joseph	2				TX
Joseph Susen	25		rents farm		
Theresie	17				
Anna	3/12				

1880 United States Census

The following is a summary of the United States Census of 1880 for Precinct 7, Austin County, Texas. This area covers the lower forks of Mill Creek, including the town of Nelsonville. The enumerator's handwriting is often very hard to read. Names are spelled as their phonetic equivalent, and the Czech and German names are nearly always misspelled. Only heads of families are listed in this summary. The "Additional # in Group" column includes those individuals who live with the family head, typically spouse, children, other family members, laborers who work on the family farm, and servants. The overwhelmingly predominant occupation of the head of household is "farmer". Family group members are listed as "keeping house", "farm labor", "laborer", "servant", or "at school". An occupation is different than these common listings is listed after the name. Individuals from the Czech lands listed their birthplace as either Bohemia, Moravia, Austria, or in some cases Prussia, such as several Shiller family members who came from Bohemia. Germans are listed as from Prussia.

Abbreviations used to denote birthplaces are:

LA = Louisiana	MS = Mississippi	VA = Virginia	KY = Kentucky
NC = North Carolina	GA = Georgia	OH = Ohio	PA = Pennsylvania
TN = Tennessee	SC = South Carolina	TX = Texas	AL = Alabama
NY = New York	DC = Dist. of Col.	B = Bohemia	M = Moravia
A = Austria	P = Prussia	E = England	SL = Scotland
SW = Switzerland	IR= Ireland	F = France	C = Canada
PL = Poland			

					Birthplace		
No.	**Head of Household**	**Race**	**Age**	**# in Group**	**Self**	**Father**	**Mother**
1	Crump, G P	W	33	2	MS	VA	VA
2	Shivil, G	B	23	1	TX	NC	AL
3	Ward, E	B	56	3	NC	NC	NC
4	Daniel,	B	45	4	GA		GA
5	Johnson, Henry (with Bouldins)	B	32	8	TX		
6	Pruitt, E	W	29	1	SC	SC	NC
7	Lee, H J	W	65	7	NC	NC	NC
8	Topscott, K C	W	38	1	MS	VA	VA
9	Lee, W B	W	32	3	NC	NC	NC
10	Gaynes, J	W	61	3	E	E	E
11	Brown,	B	50	5	LA	LA	LA
12	Ueckert, C W A	W	44	6	P	P	P
13	Wilson, W A	W	37	7	TX	KY	MS
14	Elliott	W	26	2	TX	NC	TX
15	Edgley, L	W	38	7	NC	VA	NC
16	Wells (or Mills) J W	W	29	5	NC	NC	NC
17	Manley, J S	W	32	6	AL	NC	AL
18	Breamby,	B	48	4	NC	NC	NC
19	Manly, H	W	28	5	TX	NC	AL
20	Breamby, Jesse	B	60	6	TX	AL	NC
21	Scales, E	W	48	3	TN	TN	VA
22	Logan, J W	W	42	10	AL	SC	TN
23	Houston, Sam	B	54	8	VA	VA	VA
24	Hayes, J W	W	21	2	LA	LA	LA
25	Elliott, ? P	W	26	3	TX	NC	NC
26	Bonner, Dan	B	48	6	AL	GA	GA
27	Keener, Arch	B	20	2	TX		NC
28	Bonner, David	B	20	2	TX	AL	NC

29	Howard, G Y	W	43	3	KY	NC	KY
30	Daniel, J N	W	49	8	GA	NC	NC
31	Daniel, Henry	B	45	0	GA	VA	GA
32	Bonner, Ross	B	21	3	TX	AL	AL
33	Garnett, Vinnie	B	60	6	MS	NC	NC
34	Bonner, John	Mu	25	4	TX		
35	Bonner, Aleck	B	39	9	AL	GA	GA
36	Burns, F H (Felix Huston)	W	35	6	MS	VA	NC
37	Burns, A L (Achsah Lee)	W	69	8	NC	NC	NC
38	Bar?sy, J K	W	33	2	GA	GA	GA
39	Northcross, George	W	32	7	TX		
40	Young, Henry	B	35	6	GA	GA	GA
41	Ward, R	W	45	10	NC	NC	NC
42	Watson, Joseph	W	44	5	PA	PA	PA
43	Willis, John C	W	27	2	TX	NC	AL
43	Bradley, Thomas	W	24	4	AL	GA	GA
44	Garrison, Jake	W	32	2	NC	NC	NC
45	Logan, A M	W	80	2	TN	SC	SC
46	Thompson, F M	W	39	6	AL		
47	Reason,	B	60	5	NC	NC	NC
48	Robertson, Henry	B	67	5	VA	VA	VA
49	Bradbury, ? H	W	46	10	NY	E	E
50	Thornton,	W	42	3	E	E	E
51	Chance, Henry	W	43	4	AL	SC	GA
52	Nealston, M	W	45	3	P	P	P
53	Howard, K R	W	29	2	KY	NC	SC
54	Golan, Anna	W	39	3	TX		
55	Maysie, Jacob	W	49	0	SW	SW	SW
56	Haserman, Henry	W	53	5	P	P	P
57	Howard, W R	W	33	3	KY	NC	SC
58	Elliott, F L	W	37	2	TX	NC	NC
59	Hillbolt, John	W	30	7	SW	SW	SW
60	Campbell, John	W	50	7	NC	NC	NC
61	Burns, Doss	W	29	2	TX	VA	NC
62	Dixon, George B	W	35	4	AL	SC	SC
63	Harkins, Wm	B	27	6	TX	NC	NC
64	Dixon, Debra	W	66	2	SC	SC	
SC							
	Dixon, E D (machinist)	W	23				
65	Landrum, S C (machinist)	W	46	4	AL	SC	
NC							
66	McLord, L	B	35	6	AL	SC	AL
67	Elliott, Wm	B	34	4	DC		
68	Manley, John	W	62	5	NC	NC	NC
69	Rodgers, Frank	W	30	2	TX	AL	AL
70	Garnett, H	W	50	3	AL	NC	AL
71	Garnett, Burrell	B	22	3	MS	VA	MS
72	Poole, W P	W	36	5	TN	GA	TN
73	Manley, G H	W	26	2	TX	AL	AL
74	Dabney, Dick	B	46	5	KY	VA	VA
75	Creekmore, B C	W	60	5	VA	VA	VA
76	Howard, Z T	W	26	10	TX	KY	TN
77	Voverosky, August	W	24	3	P	P	P
78	Voverosky, Fritz	W	29	3	P	P	P
79	Kauch, August	W	29	5	P	P	P
80	Elchick, John	W	44	6	TX		
81	Lott, John M	W	49	6	MS	GA	GA
82	Mayer, W C	W	36	4	P	P	P
	Baumaster, Wm (stonemason)	W					
	38						
83	Goins, M	W	27	2	AL	AL	AL
84	Bouldin, J W	W	49	9	AL	VA	VA
85	Otto, Henry	W	46	6	P	P	P
86	Blackburg, John	W	32	1	GA	GA	SC
87	Daughtry, Jarrett	W	56	2	TX	AL	KY
88	Krausse, Frank	W	23	2	P	P	P
89	Krausse, Martin	W	55	3	P	P	P
90	Younaskey, Martin	W	54	4	B	B	B
91	Molinz, Joseph	W	56	6	B	B	B
92	Shupack, John	W	62	8	B	B	B
	Zappalach, Paul (carpenter) W	50					
93	Shupack, John	W	28	2	B	B	B

94	Lindemann, A	W	39	11	P	P	P
95	Paker, Henry	W	44	5	P	P	P
96	Daughtry, Ed	W	54	12	TX	NC	KY
97	Manei (?), Frank	W	40	4	B	B	B
98	Esterrack, Joseph	W	48	7	B	B	B
99	Hadgee, August	W	35	4	P	P	P
100	Whicher, August	W	52	5	P	P	P
101	Gatenorf, Joseph	W	48	4	B	B	B
102	Pachmann, Wm	W	44	0	A	A	A
103	Hartman, Fritz	W	32	3	P	P	P
104	Wonderling, Henry	W	36	2	P	P	P
105	Mikeska, Joseph	W	30	2	A	A	A
106	Ueckert, Richard	W	32	5	P	P	P
107	Lepsyadlips (?)	W	42	6	P	P	P
108	Kaase,	W	26	4	P	P	P
109	Marman, H	W	29	5	P	P	P
110	Plausack, Joseph	W	30	6	B	B	B
111	Hendorson, Mary	B	38	3	SC	SC	SC
112	Grauender,	W	29	2	P	P	P
113	Ueckert, Gustav	W	32	4	P	P	P
114	Korgis, Gottlieb	W	57	6	P	P	P
115	Hadger, Adolph	W	28	4	P	P	P
116	Lindermann	W	31	8	P	P	P
117	Bethany, W	W	27	3	TX	AL	AL
118	Roslar, Ernst	W	43	5	P	P	P
119	Lindemann, Fritz	W	35	5	P	P	P
120	Price, George H	W	42	2	IR	IR	IR
121	Wallick, John	W	38	7	B	B	B
122	Drisgar, Joseph	W	60	2	B	B	B
123	Shiller, Anna	W	62	3	P	P	P
124	Chuslachek, Rose	W	45	2	A	A	A
125	Hinse, Frank	W	45	7	P	P	P
126	Spilhauer, Ernst	W	41	5	P	P	P
127	Rodaphgoreck (?)	W	55	2	B	B	B
128	Hoff, Fritz	W	40	6	P	P	P
129	Santack, Joseph	W	45	7	B	B	B
130	Cartlecheck, John	W	56	5	B	B	B
131	Herring, A	W	39	10	P	P	P
132	Morrish, Frank	W	50	5	B	B	B
133	Pachart, Joseph	W	35	5	B	B	B
134	Cotockcheck, Joseph	W	25	2	B	B	B
135	Hollavicks, Thomas	W	48	7	B	B	B
136	Siptak, Joseph	W	27	6	B	B	B
137	Schinchick, F	W	35	6	B	B	B
138	Poop, John	W	49	2	P	P	P
139	Shada, Frank	W	34	6	B	B	B
140	Passicka, George	W	40	8	B	B	B
141	Morse, Robert	W	40	6	P	P	P
142	Leshack, Vincent	W	47	5	B	B	B
143	Vironas, John	W	47	6	B	B	B
144	Winderchick, Joseph	W	21	2	B	B	B
145	Balusack, Frank	W	45	5	B	B	B
146	Repka, Thomas	W	38	3	A	A	A
147	Pattert, Ernst	W	40	5	P	P	P
148	Lishicar, John	W	26	3	A	A	A
149	Carlecheck, Stephan	W	47	3	A	A	A
150	Matsick, Martin	W	45	5	A	A	A
151	Ueckert, F	W	29	2	TX	P	P
152	Felker, Henry	W	64	2	P	P	P
153	Brosh, Jo	W	43	6	B	B	B
154	Hodec, Jacob	W	54	7	B	B	B
155	Rae, F	W	55	7	SL	SL	
SL							
156	Davis, Jack	B	64	2	NC	NC	NC
157	Brown, William	B	45	1	OH	PA	KY
158	Dosie, Henry	Mu	25	6	TX	TX	AL
159	Mikeska, G	W	50	5	A	A	A
160	Ceralcheck, Mike	W	28	3	P	P	P
160	Tomsic, Frank	W	44	7	P	P	P
161	? , Vincent	W	35	6	P	P	P
162	Golodcik, John	W	28	2	P	P	P
163	Kabatchka, Mat.	W	47	4	P	P	P

164	Rosner, Mattis	W	50	2	P	P	P
173	Harday, Sam	B	49	11	NC	NC	NC
174	Susan, Joseph	W	62	5	A	A	A
175	Jirasek, Joseph	W	62	5	B	B	B
176	Minton, G A	W	38	5	TX	AL	AL
177	Brown, Frank	W	35	2	NC	NC	NC
178	Bonner, Phillip	B	43	8	AL	AL	AL
179	Thompson, W A	W	45	5	AL	NC	SC
180	Milton, John	B	44	8	AL	AL	VA
182	Williamson, E C	W	46	5	GA	TN	GA
182	Bethany, Richard	B	34	5	TX	AL	AL
183	Parker, Bily	B	75	8	VA	VA	VA
184	Garrett, John	W	25	3	TX	MS	
185	Parker, John	B	20	2	TX	VA	TX
186	Shiller, Sam	W	30	4	P	P	P
187	Shiller, John	W	28	3	P	P	P
188	Nelson, John	W	30	2	NC	NC	NC
189	Hatcher, E M	W	33	5	GA	GA	GA
190	Ogg, E C	W	26	4	TX	AL	AL
191	Jackson, Farroy	B	23	2	TX	AL	AL
192	Marchack, John	W	23	1	B	B	B
193	Shiller, John	W	66	5	P	P	P
194	Mosley, John	B	28	5	LA	LA	AL
195	Shiller, John Jr.	W	31	3	P	P	P
196	Ford, Peter	B	49	9	AL	SC	GA
197	Burgess, Wm	W	57	5	TN	E	AL
198	Mikeska, Rose	W	63	1	B	B	B
199	Osnitz, John	W	25	2	B	B	B
200	Malow, L H	W	63	7	GA	GA	GA
201	Yaukets, George	W	49	5	A	A	A
202	Kramolis, Joseph	W	60	4	A	A	A
203	Feldar, Joseph	W	50	4	B	B	B
204	Paverlick, John	W	42	7	A	A	A
205	Christoff, Frank	W	34	8	B	B	B
206	Johnson, G	B	43	5	TX	AL	AL
207	Baggett, William	W	37	6	NC	NC	NC
208	Onrsheck, Frank	W	51	4	B	B	B
209	Daushack, Vincent	W	25	1	B	B	B
210	Bethany, J W	W	56	6	AL	AL	AL
211	Bartta, Wesley	B	35	3	AL	AL	AL
212	Vinkliss, Joseph	W	26	3	AL	AL	AL
213	Mitiska, John	W	25	4	A	A	A
214	Baggett, Sam	W	28	2	NC	NC	NC
215	Marchak, Frank	W	29	2	B	B	B
216	Ward, Richard	B	50	1	AL	AL	AL
217	Marchak, Joseph	W	26	3	B	B	B
218	Charnosky, Frank	W	50	6	B	B	B
219	Ogg, John	W	48	3	GA	GA	GA
220	Janota, John	W	24	1	B	B	B
221	Leshica, John	W	45	5	B	B	B
222	Doller, Mat	B	65	5	TN	VA	PA
223	Jar (?), Joseph	W	24	0	AL	SC	GA
224	Shelburn, (Mary) Catherine	W	47	9	AL	SC	AL
225	Shelburne, John (2nd, son of MC)	W	24	1	TX	AL(TN)	AL
226	Havline, Harrison	B	48	4	AL		AL
227	Murrick, J	W	36	6	B	B	B
228	Oppiveh, Jo	W	32	5	B	B	B
229	Kamas, John	W	41	6	B	B	B
230	Kovosh, Paul	W	34	5	B	B	B
231	Yaukits, Martin	W	51	7	B	B	B
232	Rosher, August	W	44	4	P	P	P
233	Matejeka, John	W	38	6	B	B	B
234	Ballitka, John	W	65	2	B	B	B
235	Christoff, Matt	W	39	5	B	B	B
236	Driveronick, John	W	25	1	TX	B	B
237	Shiller, Charles	W	46	4	B	B	B
238	Shaveeck, John	W	45	6	B	B	B
239	Siptak, Frank	W	24	2	B	B	B
240	Danayoufrack, Thomas	W	62	5	M	M	M
241	Zafecick, Martin	W	56	2	B	B	B
242	Holck, Joseph	W	50	7	M	M	M
243	Settle, Gustav	W	34	7	P	P	P

244	Shu (?), Stephan	W	65	5	B	B	B
245	Meichamann, H	W	34	3	P	P	P
246	Jackson, Albert	B	46	8	MS	MS	MS
247	Flake, Ferrell	B	38	8	MS	VA	VA
248	Rollwing, Otto	W	18	2	TX	P	P
249	Schonovagle, A	W	46	5	P	P	P
250	Creekmore, Albert	W	29	2	KY	KY	TN
251	Mikiska, Frank	W	25	1	B	B	B
252	Bavcicia, John	W	38	6	B	B	B
253	Dozark, John	W	75	1	B	B	B
254	King, Francis	B	25	4	TX	VA	VA
	Botaska, Joseph	W	23	6	TX	B	B
255	Klohn, Fred	W	44	7	P	P	P
256	Settle, Fritz	W	24	2	P	P	P
257	Breamby, Bill	B	33	5	AL	AL	NC
258	Wallis, Dick	B	26	1	TX	AL	AL
259	Wanner, James	B	70	3	VA	VA	VA
260	Logn, John C	W	32	3	AL	TN	AL
261	Elliott, Elias	W	61	6	NC	NC	NC
262	Mischnowsky, Aug (blacksmith)	W	43	3	P	P	P
263	Willis, Joseph	W	56	8	NC	NC	NC
264	James, Tobe	W	30	4	NC	NC	NC
265	Dancer, Henry	B	27	2	TX	AL	AL
266	Burns, N (Napolean) (merchant)	W	35	3	TX	NC	
NC							
267	Mikeska, John	W	46	2	B	B	B
	Hubbart, Peter (painter)						
268	Gartner, Joh	W	48	3	F	P	P
269	Gendnian, Paul (blacksmith)	W	42	4	C	C	
C							
270	Langer, Rose	W	39	4	B	B	B
271	Lewis, Isaac (farmer)	W	44	11	PL	PL	
PL							
272	Bethany, James W (lawyer)	W	30	10	TX	AL	
AL							
273	Jackson, Sol	B	28	4	TX	MS	AL
274	Miller, Henry (wheelwright)	W	27	2	TX	P	
P							
275	Lewis, B (merchant)	W	26	2	PL	PL	PL
	Wolf, A (merchant)	W	25		PL	PL	PL
	Coehn, Isaac (merchant)	W	27		PL	PL	
PL							
276	Brinson, Peter	B	27	1	AL	AL	AL
277	Foster, G W (physician)	W	45	8	IL	KY	KY
278	Thompson, Robert (physician)	W	37	4	AL	AL	AL
279	Tison, A G	W	54	4	AL	AL	AL
280	Morro, Fritz	W	39	3	TX	B	B
281	Miller, Joachim	W	33	2	TX	B	B
282	Ivey, H	W	36	11	GA	AL	SC

1900 United States Census

The following listing represents all the heads of households as listed in the Federal Census of 1900 for those who were recorded in Nelsonville, Austin County, Texas, by enumerator J. A. Malechek on June 1 through June 20, 1900.

No.	Head of Family	Immig.	Race	Occupation	Birth Date	Self	Birthplace Father	Number in group
1	Malechec, J.	1860	W	Farmer	9/1859	Aus	Boh	12
2	Schmidt, C.		W	Teacher	8/1869	Tex	Ger	6
3	Haedge, Charles	1855	W	Farmer	1/1837	Ger	Ger	7
4	Mikeska, Frank		W	Farmer	3/1870	Tex	Boh	3
5	Hill, Duglas		B	Farmer	6/1875	Tex	Tex	3
6	Adamek, Stephan	1894	W	Farmer	5/1853	Boh	Boh	9
7	Sailer, A.		W	Farmer	5/1854	Tex	Ger	7
8								
9	Glaser, Robert	1871	W	Farmer	1/1865	Ger	Ger	9
10	Leps, Gottlieb	1870	W	Farmer	7/1839	Ger	Ger	5
11	Schupak, M (?)		W		10/1861	Boh	Boh	7
12	Janosky, Joseph	1870	W	Farmer	1/1865	Boh	Boh	8
13	Bethe, Herman	1870	W	Farmer	8/1864	Boh	Boh	9
14	Kasparek, John	1883	W	Farmer	5/1868	Boh	Boh	6
15	Janosky, Frank	1883	W	Farmer	9/1858	Boh	Boh	8
16	Bravenec, John	1880	W	Farmer	3/1870	Boh	Boh	5
17	Watushek, Frank	1884	W	Farmer	9/1874	Boh	Boh	4
18	Chernosky, Ignac		W	Farmer	10/1871	Tex	Boh	3
19	Div(?)oky, Franz	1882	W	Farmer	9/1836	Boh	Boh	2
20	Matejka, Frank	1879	W	Merchant	7/1866	Boh	Boh	8
21	Walechek, Ad.		W	Farmer	8/1870	Tex	Boh	4
22	Kroulik, John		W	Physician	12/1872	Tex	Boh	2
23	McGregor, J.C.		W	Physician	1855	NC	NC	4
24	Minton, A.		W	Farmer	1839	MS	?	2
25	Barthy?			Farmer		Tex		5
26	Shembera, Mary	1896	W	Laundress	1/1865	Boh	Boh	5
27	Willis, George		W	Farmer	2/1858	Tex	NC	2
28	Meissner, Martha		W	Farmer	3/1860	Tex	Ger	6
29	Koukol, Alouis	1891	W	Clergyman	9/1869	Boh	Boh	4

30	Korenek, John 1870	W Blacksmith	10/1867	Boh	Boh	4
31	Kan(?)ak, Thomas 1883	W Farmer	8/1856	Boh	Boh	6
32	Watushek, Frank 1886	W Farmer	3/1847	Boh	Boh	4
33	Blazek, Ignac 1884	W Farmer	6/1848	Boh	Boh	8
34	Sepcik, Frank 1894	W Farmer	6/1860	Boh	Boh	3
35	Blazek, John 1889	W Farmer	8/1877	Boh	Boh	2
36	Koppa, Josef 1869	W Farmer	5/1867	Boh	Boh	3
37	Olsen, (?) 1870	W Farmer	7/1860	Den	Den	3
38	Shelburn, John P.	W Farmer	8/1869	Tex	Ala	7
39	Hubert, (?)	W Farmer	10/1859	Tex	Swtz	6
40	K (?) 1884	W Farmer		Boh	Boh	9
41	Bacica, J. (?) 1875	W Farmer	5/1872	Boh	Boh	1
42	Clinger (?)	B Farmer	9/1859	Tex	?	2
43	Janosky, John 1883	W Farmer	6/1862	Boh	Boh	5
44	Barthy, A.	W Farmer	1889	Boh	Boh	2
45	Chernosky, Wilhemina	W Farmer	1871	Tex	Boh	5
46	Dayvis, Will	B (?)	5/1883	Tex	Tex	4
47	Golan, Anna	W Farmer	1830	Boh	Boh	4
48	Mikeska, Frank 1854	W Farmer	10/1854	Boh	Boh	4
49	Maresh, John 1866	W Farmer	1830	Boh	Boh	4
50	Maresh, Joseph	W Farmer	4/1877	Tex	Boh	3
51	Maresh, Winc 1866	W Farmer	5/1864	Boh	Boh	8
52	Maresh, Willy	W Farmer	12/1868	Tex	Boh	2
53	Burbask (?), John 1883	W Farmer	1843	Boh	Boh	3
54	Burbask (?)	 Farmer		Boh	Boh	3
55	Daughtry, Edward	W Farmer	10/1824	Tex	Tenn	10
56	Houza (?), Frank 1889	W Farmer	12/1869	Boh	Boh	8
57	Janosky, John 1884	W Farmer	1/1865	Boh	Boh	6
58	Chernosky, John 1871	W Farmer	3/1869	Boh	Boh	7
59	Bednar, Frank 1880	W Farmer	8/1864	Boh	Boh	2
60	Siptak, Jos.	W Farmer	7/1875	Tex	Boh	3
61	Sa (?) 1889	W Farmer	5/1872	Boh	Boh	6
62	Wanderling (?) 1872	W (?)		Ger	Ger	3
63	Fick 1891	W Farmer				
64	Mockel(?), Edward 1853	W Farmer	1/1849	Ger	Ger	8
65	Kuckua, Paul 1880	W (?)	8/1873	`Tex	Boh	5

66	Plashek, John 1881	W Farmer	5/1874	Boh	Boh	6
67	Adameck, Thomas 1892	W Farmer	6/1946	Boh	Boh	6
68	Schultz, Paul 1892	W Farmer	9/1874	Ger	Ger	3
69	Schroeder. John 1870	W Farmer	10/1830	Ger	Ger	3
70	Kudlachek, John 1870	W Farmer	10/1867	Boh	Boh	5
71	Halian, John 1892	W Farmer	4/1871	Boh	Boh	3
72	Haedge, Adolph 1856	W Farmer	1851	Ger	Ger	2
73	Schiller, Joseph 1880	W Farmer	5/1856	Boh	Boh	9
74	Maresh, Franz 1871	W Farmer	3/1829	Boh	Boh	2
75	Susan, John Jr. 6	W	6/1875	Tex	Boh	
76	Wickes, Bernard 1869	W Farmer	2/1854	Ger	Ger	7
77	Schmoroder, Fritz 1883	W Farmer	9/1858	Ger	Ger	9
78	Meissner, George	W Teacher	3/1878	Tex	Ger	4
79	Kuchera, John 1872	W Farmer	12/1864	Boh	Boh	6
80	Kuchera, Josef 1872	W Farmer	3/1835	Boh	Boh	2
81	Mikeska, Thomas 1888	W Farmer	6/1880	Boh	Boh	4
82	Plashek, Josef 1881	W Farmer	1871	Boh	Boh	2
83	Susan, John	W Farmer		Tex	Boh	8
84	Rosenbaum, Billy 1884	W Farmer	2/1866	Ger	Ger	5
85	Braun, Les 1883	W Farmer	9/1865	Ger	Ger	8
86	Wetzel, Gottfried 1872	W Farmer	9/1849	Ger	Ger	7
87	Flake, Terrell	B Farmer	5/1840	Miss	Miss	7
88	Albert, Otto	W Farmer	6/1863	Tex	Ger	9
89	Shimara, Josef	W Farmer	4/1857	Tex	Boh	6
90	Derssjanek (?) 1855	W Farmer		Boh	Boh	8
91	Walchik, John 1888(?) (?)	W	12/1865	Boh	Boh	7
92	Mikeska, Josef 1889	W Farmer	12/1877	Boh	Boh	4
93	Maglik, Josef 1897	W Farmer	2/1866	Boh	Boh	2
94	Roesler, August (?)	W Farmer	2/1836	Ger	Ger	5
95	Zettle, Fritz (?)	W Farmer	8/1856	Ger	Ger	10
96	Glaeser, Ernst 1858	W Farmer	3/1851	Ger	Ger	5
97	Machemehl, Otto	W Farmer	6/1853	Tex	Ger	9
98	Slechik (?), John 1870	W Farmer		Boh	Boh	4
99	Lesek (?)	W Farmer				4
100	Shupak, John 1855	W Farmer	8/1850	Boh	Boh	8
101	Siptak, Annie 1870	W Farmer	2/1857	Boh	Boh	4

102	Schovaisa, Frank 1894	W Farmer	9/1855	Boh	Boh	5
103	Shiska, Frank 1884	W Farmer	10/1865	Boh	Boh	8
104	Pshencik, John 1880	W Farmer	11/1847	Boh	Boh	3
105	Slacik, Kathy 1888	W Farmer	5/1860	Boh	Boh	1
106	Herrvol (?), John 1883	W	2/1852	Boh	Boh	2
107	Schvoboda, Frank 1884	W Farmer	10/1857	Boh	Boh	11
108	Krause, Herman 1870	W Farmer	5/1860	Ger	Ger	10
109	Peshek, John	W Farmer	6/1859	Tex	Boh	6
110	Shiller, John 1853	W Farmer	7/1852	Boh	Boh	5
111	Shiller, W 1854	W Farmer	10/1850	Boh	Boh	15
112	Chlapek, John 1884	W Farmer	5/1870	Boh	Boh	4
113	P (?) 1882	W Farmer		Boh	Boh	7
114	Micka, Frank 1883	W Farmer	5/1854	Boh	Boh	7
115	Mikeska, George 1884	W Farmer	12/1864	Boh	Boh	6
116	Ueckert. Otto	W Farmer	5/1877	Tex	Tex	3
117	Mikeska, John	W Farmer	6/1867	Tex	Boh	4
118	Robertson, Henry	B Farmer	4/1874	Tex	Tex	5
119	Peter, Henry 1895	W Farmer	2/1857	Ger	Ger	6
120	Brown, Jake	W Farmer	8/1868	Tex	(?)	10
121	S(?)ander, Lorena	W Farmer		Tex	Ger	8
122	T(?)eske, Albert 1863	W Farmer	4/1841	Ger	Ger	6
123	Holth, Willie 1890	W Farmer	6/1870	Ger	Ger	5
124	Kovar, John 1873	W Farmer	6/1836	Boh	Boh	3
125	Macek, Thomas 1874	W Farmer	2/1870	Boh	Boh	6
126	Brast (?) Josef 1873	W Farmer	11/1839	Boh	Boh	7
127	Slovak, Steven 1877	W Farmer	8/1869	Boh	Boh	4
128	Slovak, Rosina 1877	W Farmer	6/1832	Boh	Boh	3
129	Willam, Fritz	W Farmer	4/1854	Tex	In. Terr.	6
130	Bonner, Robert	B		Tex	Ala	2
131	(?) 1883	Farmer		Ger	Ger	5
132	Lesh, Christoph 1874	W Farmer	2/1861	Ger	Ger	6
133	Fick, William 1883	W Farmer	8/1853	Ger	Ger	6
134	Hoffman, Donald 1887	W Farmer	9/1869	Ger	Ger	4
135	Falle, Franz 1896	W Farmer	12/1871	Ger	Ger	2
136	Hering, Otto	W Farmer	2/1864	Tex	Ger	13
137	L (?), Henry 1868	W Farmer	2/1865	Ger	Ger	6

138	Holke, Karl	W Farmer	1/1872	Tex	Ger	4
139	Huffmann, Hugo 1884	W Farmer	1834	Ger	Ger	5
140	(?)					4
141	Stefan, Vinc 1888	W Farmer	4/1870	Tex	Boh	7
142	Robertson, Locket	B Farmer	11/1874	Tex	(?)	10
143	Shelburn, John P.	W Farmer	2/1851	Tex	Miss (TN)	5
144	Jackson, Funtroy	B Farmer	5/1858	Tex	(?)	10
145	Daughtry, Alvina 1882	W Landlord	5/1856	Boh	Boh	3
146	D(?)ette, Carl 1881	W Farmer		Ger	Ger	5
147	Esterak, John 1872	W Farmer		Boh	Boh	6
148	(?)					
149	Bacica, John Sr. 1869	W Farmer	1/1838	Boh	Boh	3
150	Smith, Newton	B Farmer	1/1830	Ky	Vir	7
151	Wernly, Jacob 1888	W Farmer	8/1868	Swtz	Swtz	5
152	Wernly, Sam 1889	W Farmer	3/1872	Swtz	Swtz	3
153	Meury, Sam 1883	W Farmer	4/1870	Swtz	Swtz	4
154	Jurcka, John 1883	W Farmer	3/1861	Boh	Boh	7
155	Petrusek, John 1887	W Farmer	9/1871	Boh	Boh	7
156	Maresh, Frank 1882	W Farmer	11/1871	Boh	Boh	3
157	Kasparek, Frank 1884	W Farmer	2/1874	Boh	Boh	5
158	Esterak, (?)	W Farmer	3/1860	Boh	Boh	1
159	Will, (?)	B Farmer		Tex	Ky	5
160	Drizgr (?), Frank 1880	W Farmer	12/1837	Boh	Boh	8
161	Kuty, Martin 1885	W Farmer	1/1843	Boh	Boh	6
162	Kamas, (?) 1874	W Farmer	1/1846	Boh	Boh	7
163	Holt, August	W Farmer	5/1859	Tex	Ger	10
164	Terry, Harrison	B Farmer	12/1829	Ga	Ga	8
165	Wilke, Otto	W Farmer		Tex	Ger	2
166	Jurgens, Paul	W Farmer		Tex	Ger	4
167	(?) 1891	Farmer		Boh	Boh	2
168	(?)					1
169	(?)					2
170	Kamas, Thomas 1884	W Farmer	2/1845	Boh	Boh	6
171	Beran, John 1882	W Farmer	9/1876	Boh	Boh	6
172	Shelburn, Samuel (Allen)	W Landlord	7/1817	Tenn	Vir	2
173	Milton, John	B Farmer	3/1845	Ala	Ala	6
174	Balousek, Frank 1884	W Farmer	3/1850	Boh	Boh	10

175	Hicks, George	B Farmer	12/1877	Tex	Tex	5
176	Kalarek, Stephan 1894	W Farmer	3/1861	Boh	Boh	6
177	Bradbury, H.	W Farmer	1/1872	Tex	NY	7
178	Kanak, John 1886	W Farmer	8/1872	Boh	Boh	1
179	Janosky, Josef 1884	W Farmer	2/1866	Boh	Boh	7
180	Mikeska, (?) 1884	W Farmer		Boh	Boh	3
181	Maresh, (?) 1888	W Farmer		Boh	Boh	3
182	Mikeska, John 1884	W Farmer	3/1874	Boh	Boh	8
183	Machat, Josef 1883	W Farmer	3/1854	Boh	Boh	9
184	Shefchik, Frank 1883	W Farmer	1863	Boh	Boh	7
185	Machemehl, C. F.	W Farmer	3/1857	Tex	Ger	7
186	Bravenec, Thomas 1881	W Farmer	5/1872	Boh	Boh	4
187	Helarek (?) 1894	W Farmer	2/1869	Boh	Boh	5
188	Daniels, Allen	B Farmer	1/1837	Ga	Ga	5
189	Hinze, Frank 1866	W Farmer	12/1835	Ger	Ger	6
190	Esterak, Josef 1872	W Farmer	3/1858	Boh	Boh	8
191	Sebesta, Annie 1879	W Farmer	1/1835	Boh	Boh	7
192	Layner, Lara	W Farmer	8/1856	NY	NY	8
193	Burns, John	W Farmer	5/1844	Tex		9
194	Jackson, H.	B Farmer		Tex	(?)	8
195	Wallis (?)	 Farmer		Tex	(?)	5
196	Hynes, Lizzie	B Farmer	3/1855	Ala	(?)	9
197	Daniels, W.	B Farmer	8/1861	Tex	(?)	9
198	Holba, Josef 1883	W Farmer	5/1855	Boh	Boh	7
199	Sheda (?), Frank 1876	W Farmer	5/1842	Boh	Boh	5
200	Shefchik, John 1883	W Farmer	10/1870	Boh	Boh	2
201	Blazek, Frank 1883	W Farmer	4/1875	Boh	Boh	5
202	G(?)acik, Josef 1884	W Farmer	7/1854	Boh	Boh	9
203	Wenny, Sam	B Farmer	2/1849	SC	SC	7
204	Hampton, W.	B Day Labor	5/1869	Tex	Tex	6
205	Burton, Jack	B Farmer	1/1855	Tex	Tex	4
206	Anclins(?), John	B Farmer	1/1873	Tex	(?)	4
207	Huchlik, J. 1882	W Farmer	5/1850	Boh	Boh	2
208	H (?), Lara	W Dressmakr	5/1850	Al	SC	2
209	Jechec, C.	W Farmer	1827	Tex	Boh	6
210	(?)	 Farmer				4

211	Cuberson, George	B Farmer	5/1855	Tex	Ala	8
212	Garnet, Thomas	B Farmer	3/1872	Tex	Ala	8
213	Marshal, John	B	2/1871	Tex	Tex	2
214	Doharns(?) 1871	W Farmer	8/1852	Ger	Ger	10
215	Reason, Willy	B Farmer	1/1866	Tex	(?)	6
216	Bolden, Lymas	B Farmer	7/1874	Tex	Tex	5
217	Logan, J.	W Farmer	11/1837	Ala	SC	8
218	Garnett, Robert	B Farmer	9/1869	Tex	Miss	9
219	(?)	 Day Labor				2
220	Bonner, Daniel	B Farmer	6/1838	Ala	Ga	4
221	Bonner, Alex	B Farmer	2/1869	Tex	Ala	2
222	Keener, Arthur	B Farmer	5/1860	Tex	(?)	11
223	Bravenec, John 1880	W Farmer	3/1835	Boh	Boh	5
224	Oslica, Paul 1893	W Farmer	5/1866	Boh	Boh	3
225	Koppa, Thomas 1877	W Farmer	2/1869	Boh	Boh	7
226	Hill, Alan	W	1/1882	Tex	Tex	3
227	Manly, John	B Farmer	3/1876	Tex	Ala	5
228	Garnett, S	B	1/1875	Tex	Vir	2
229	Lee, W.R.	W Farmer	12/1849	NC	NC	14
	Dolezal, Alvin	W Blacksmth	2/1872	Tex	Boh	
230	Ueckert, Paul	W Farmer	10/1860	Tex	Ger	6
231	Brimbry, Pilgrim	B Farmer	1/1845	NC	NC	12
232	Johnson, H.	B Farmer	1/1850	Tex	(?)	4
233	Hardman, Anthony 1882	W Farmer	1/1855	Ger	Ger	7
234	(?) 2		 Farmer			
235	Andreas 1867	W Farmer		Ger	Ger	7
236	Mikeska, Josef	W Farmer	9/1864	Tex	Boh	5
237	Bethany, Richard	B Farmer	1/1845	Tex	Ala	10
238	Huchlick, Frank 1882	W Farmer	1/1862	Boh	Boh	4
239	Cermak, John 1893	W Farmer	9/1854	Boh	Boh	4
240	Hien, Edward	W Farmer	3/1873	Tex	Tex	8
241	Uhrik, John 1877	W Farmer	1/1856	Boh	Boh	9
242	Shiller, Charles	W Farmer	1/1865	Tex	Boh	10
243	Janecek, Wilm..	W Farmer	11/1857	Tex	Boh	7
244	Chernosky, R. 1873	W	1/1842	Boh	Boh	4
245	Kedlecek, R. 1871	W Farmer	1839	Boh	Boh	1

246	E(?) 1856	W Farmer		Boh	Boh	7
247	(?)	 Farmer				4
248	Miller, J.	W Farmer	1/1831	Tex	Ger	6
249	Bonner, (?)	B Farmer	1/1835	Ala	Ala	10
250	Bonner, Will	B Farmer	7/1872	Tex	Ala	4
251	Pavelka, John 1866	W Farmer	3/1866	Boh	Boh	5
252	Welburn, Emma	W Farmer	5/1859	Tex	Ger	7
253	Pavelka, Frank	W Farmer	3/1871	Tex	Boh	5
254	Pavelka, (?) 1866	W Farmer	1/1845	Boh	Boh	7
255	Ebert, Charles	W Farmer		Aus	Aus	2
256	(?)					1
257	(?)					2

Note: The number listed in each group includes spouse, children at home, other relatives and servants and boarders.

Appendix 1: Land Ownership

Using the land plat filed by Guy M. Bryan on 17 April, 1855, as a guide, the ownership of land in the Nelsonville area prior to 1900 is listed as follows, with reference to the seller, buyer, acerage, price and date of sale. The reference to the Volume and first page in the Deed Records of Austin County, Texas, is indicated in parentheses as (Vol, Page). The plat is in (IJ/156).

Steven F. Austin Four Leagues: Granted 15 Jan 1830 (74/286)
Lower (Eastern Division) of Steven F. Austin Four Leagues: Platted 17 April 1855 (Vol. I-J Page 156)

Date	Deed Record	Buyer	Seller	Acres	Price
Lot Number 1 - 898 acres					
2 JUN 1833		H.N. Cleveland	J.F. Pease	200 (Lot 1W)	
29 DEC 1842	(B/48)	David Ayres	H.H. Cleveland	1000	
7 AUG 1839	(B/48)	David Hedden	David Ayers	1000	
15 JUN 1847	(C/)	Heddon and Day	David Ayres		
20 NOV 1847		Micajah Terry	David Ayres	part of 898 acres	
6 SEP 1845	(C/47)		Ayres of Center Hill		
	(DE/36)	Rufus E. Campbell	H.N. Cleveland est.	307	
	(8/553)	W.S. Shiller		35	
	(M/528)	W. S. Shiller		6	
	(I/413)	Gottfried Andreas	219		
11 DEC 1893	(14/550)	Thomas Koppa	Herman Andreas 30	370	
24 MAY 1912	(41/561)	Thomas Koppa	Jocac	15	225
14 MAY 1866	(L/607)	Wm. A. Thompson	Heddin Estate	25	163
1 DEC 1865	(L/344)	Wm. A. Thompson	Heddin Estate	215	
Lot Number 2 - 409 acres					
14 NOV 1865	(M/93)	W.W. Nichols	L.H. McNelly(Wash Co)	151	500
14 NOV 1865	(M/20)	M. Terry	L.H. McNelly 270		
10 MAR 1873	(7/551)	Sadie Shiller (Aus Co)	W.W. Nichols	151	3200
10 OCT 1881	(20/538)	W.S. Shiller	E. M. Hatcher	100	
	(20/540)	J.S. Shiller		88	
Lot Number 4 - 409 acres					
1 APR 1851	(F/149)	Elias Elliot	Geo. Grimes Estate	165	331
26 NOV 1865	(L/318)	Ransom G. Burns	Richardson, Day, Giddings	409	1432
1 OCT 1884	(5/474)				
7 JAN 1887	(5/475)	Felix Burns	John and Rosa Burns	66	1300
	66 acres later called homestead tract of Ransom Burns, left to John & Rosa Burns				
27 NOV 1905	(31/304)	W. Samuel Shiller	estate of Achsah Burns	209	2438
31 DEC 1887	(8/315)	George Koppa	Felix H. Burns	66	1430
15 DEC 1890	(10/447)	Thomas Koppa	George & Anna Kopa	66	1440
13 JAN 1872	(Q/557)	Felix H. Burns	R.G. Burns	57	1000
4 NOV 1883	(2/204)	J.P. Wells	Felix H. Burns	57	1150
7 AUG 1893	(14/182)	Wm. Breambry	F. H. Burns	57	900
	(Burns evidentally forclosed on note to Wells, regaining 57 acres then selling to Breambry)				
30 OCT 1872	(T/606)	John W. Lott	R.G. Burns	40	359
17 JAN 1866	(L/680)	Aaron M. Logan	R.G. Burns	25	87
	(20/139)	Samuel Shiller		12	
1 JAN 1874	(S525)	John Burns	Ransom Burns	66	3000

29 OCT 1875	(U/271)	John Burns	Achsah Burns	66	1500

Achsah Burns was widow of Ransom G. Burns. Children of Achsah & R.G. were Joanna, F.H., N.?, Narcissa Ward, Mary Ann, Daniel, Nancy, and E.H.

<u>Lot No. 6 - 1030 acres</u>

8 JUN 1848	(DE/46)	James W. Bethany	Guy M. Bryan	156	
8 MAR 1850	(DE/94)	Wm. Norcross	Guy M. Bryan	180	180
25 AUG 1852	(F/151)	Elias Elliot	Guy M. Bryan	694	694
3 JAN 1854	(F/411)	Jasper N. Daniel	Elias Elliot	200	1000
29 OCT 1856	(IJ/614)	E.C. Williamson	Elias Elliot	87	100
30 AUG 1879	(3/508)	Joseph Watson	E.C. Williamson	43	427
8 OCT 1880	(X/222)	Isaac Lewis	F.L. Elliot		1775
31 AUG 1882	(Z/22)	James S. Manley	Wm. Norcross	180	3000
24 Feb 1890	(9/411)	Charles Estarak			
18 APR 1891	(11/351)	Jan Bravenec	J. O. Manley	103	2064
14 JUN 1893	(14/25)	E.G. Steck	James S. Manley	144	3575
19 JAN 1898	(21/78)	Arch Keener	Isaac Lewis	30	390
5 DEC 1898	(21/299)	Jan Bravenec	E. G. Steck	144	2500
10 AUG 1883	(1/289)	J.S. Manley	Mary Williamson	47	400
(Jordan Bonner timber tract adjoining Wm. Norcross place)					
		Edmund Ward		45	
	(F/163)	Joseph Macat		164	
		Frank Plasek		100	
		John Bravenec		124	
16 NOV 1869	(O/245)	Daniel Bonner	Sarah Elliot	80	500
29 DEC 1882	(Z/336)	Daniel Bonner	Isaac Lewis	45	500

<u>Lot No. 8 - 507 acres</u>

13 SEP 1852	(F/163)	Daniel Harris	Guy M. Bryan	507	1016
8 APR 1853	(F/195)	Jasper N. Daniel	Daniel Harris	507	2031
29 DEC 1873	(S/436)	J. W. Bethany et al	Jasper Daniel	78	2825
16 JUL 1873	(S/161)	Daniel Bonner	Jasper Daniel	47	1055
31 DEC 1872	(R/697)	J. S. Manley	J. N. Daniel	124+70	5200
4 SEP 1878	(V/461)	Sam Houston, Sr.	J. N. Daniel	49	1000
19 JUL 1878	(V/538)	John Bonner	J. W. Bethany	35	250
25 SEP 1880	(X/403)	John Garrett	J. N. Daniel	35	750
23 JUL 1893	(S/167)	M. Terry	J.N. Daniel	100	
13 DEC 1855	(IJ/530)	John P. Atchinson	J.N. Daniel	23	
6 NOV 1880	(X/344)	Allen Daniel		18	
		John H. Campbell		21	

<u>Lot No. 10 - 484 acres</u>

9 MAR 1849	(DE 64)	John P. Shelbourne buys a town lot in Bellville.			
15 APR 1857	(G/13)	John P. Atchinson	Guy M. Bryan	605,part #9	1745
13 DEC 1855	(IJ/557)	J. N. Daniel	J.P. Atchinson	50	
	(34/402)	Joseph Holba		50	
25 OCT 1880	(X/345)	Oscar Elliot	Jasper P. Atchinson	103	1000
	(55/429)	John Sefcik		82	

<u>Lot No. 11 - 1040 acres</u>

3 MAR 1859	(H/191)	Jasper N. Daniel	M. Austin Bryan	1040	
14 NOV 1865	(L/363)	C.W.A. Ueckert	J.N. Daniel et ux	1040	5500

<u>Lot No. 9 - 547 acres</u>

3 MAY 1847	(IJ/227)	J.N. Daniel	E. M. Pease	100	
3 MAY 1847	(IJ/227)	E. M. Pease	James F. Perry	740	
30 NOV 1852		J. N. Daniel	E. M. Pease	740	
28 MAY 1859	(H/319)	Loftin Reddick	Jasper Daniel	100	

18 JAN 1858	(G/237)	Wyatt M. Brooks	Jasper Daniel	100	debt
15 APR 1857	(G/13)	John P. Atkinson	Guy M. Bryan	93	
	(14/360)	John Burns		10	
9 APR 1888	(7/260)	John Burns	J. H. Machemehl 10	149	
4 APR 1882	(Y/441)	J.H. Machemehl	J. Saynor	47	
13 JAN 1879	(W/111)	W.R. Lee	James Saynor	100	1000
	(27/280)	Frank Sebesta			
19 NOV 1895	(17/155)	Frank & Jos. Sebesta	Paul Machemehl	150	450
	(F/337)	James Saynor	George W. Breeding	347	
	(27/542)	K.R. Howard		138	
	(31/256)	Tom Bravenec		133	
	(43/151)	Tom Bravenec		36	
	(13/106)	Paul Machemehl		100	
	(12/413)	Paul Machemehl		100	

<u>Lot No. 7 - 640 acres</u>

28 JAN 1854	(F/423)	Thomas Flake	John Ward	228	$2700
	(33/24)	Chas. Machemehl	Paul Machemehl		
	(39/145)	Chas. Sebesta		152	
		W.L. Shelborn		154	
		Chas. F. Machemehl		102	
		Thomas Bravenec	P. & C.F. Machemehl	60	

11 MAR 1865 (T/361) Jane Thompson estate to R.W. Thompson, Margaret Willis, Isabel Daughtry, W.A. Thompson & George Foster (for minor children Charles & Fannie Foster).

11 NOV 1882	(Z/142)	R. W. Thompson	A. T. Lynn	453	7000
13 NOV 1915	(48/527)	George Mikeska	R. W. Thompson	453	
16 FEB 1942	(136/306)	Geo. Mikeska Jr.	Geo. Mikeska Sr.	105	
	(136/493)	Jerry J. Mikeska	Geo. Mikeska Sr.	126	
	(50/551)	John Mikeska	Geo. Mikeska	157	
		John Surovik		24	

<u>Lot No. 5 - 616 acres</u>

4 OCT 1851		Jane Thompson	Sam G. Kuykendall	616	
		F.M. Thompson		138	
		R.W. Thompson			
30 JAN 1878	(V/460)	Oscar Elliot	J. W. Terry	118	1000
	(29/551)	Geo. Mikeska	R.W. Thomopson 38		
	(138/623)	Joe A. Mikeska	Geo. Mikeska	123	
	(16/148)	Geo. Mikeska	C.C. & Fannie Foster	105	
		Frank Uhrik		24	
	(50/551)	John Mikeska	George Mikeska	23	
	(18/495)	Jos. F. Janovsky	G.T. Willis et al	70	
	(34/388)	John Slacik	G.T. Willis et al	190	

Middle of Steven F. Austin Four Leagues

<u>Lot No. 4 - 562 acres</u>

8 JUN 1848	(DE/46)	James W. Bethany	Guy M. Bryan	562

<u>Lot 3 - 650 acres</u>

24 JAN 1845	A.M. Logan	Sam Kuykendall	125
21 DEC 1850	John Manley	Sam Kuykendall	525

Manley then of Walker Co. TX.

George Grimes League: Granted March 16, 1831 (Vol 3 page 322; Vol. 7 page 10; and Vol. 10 page 141).
Benjamin Eaton League: Granted May 16, 1827. (Vol. 3 page 56; Vol. 10 page 140)

Related Records:

12 DEC 1850 John Campbell to Solomon Ward, 150 acres on the East fork of Mill Creek, part of the Hodge land (presumably the grant above Kuykendall near Welcome).

29 SEP 1848 Hodge to Sam P. Shelborn, 500 acres in Washington County abutting Compton, Barnhill and Glenn. (DE/229)

24 JAN 1845 Sam G. Kuykendall to A.M. Logan, 125 acres in Lot 3 that Kuykendall bought of Alex Somerville, being at the southeast corner of 50 acres sold to John Bell.

28 NOV 1844 D.F. Perry to E.A. Pease, 1198 acres for $1348, bounded by Mrs. Kuykendall, west by Georgfe Carothers, South by West Fork of Mill Creek and east by J.P. Shelborn.

21 OCT 1837 Bryant Daughtry from Von Roeder and Amsler, 2/3 league on West waters of Mill Creek 15 miles from San Felipe.

29 MAR 1839 J. Benton Johnson and H.N. Cleveland divided Lots 2 and 4 adjacent to the lands of George Grimes.

4 DEC 1849 Guy Bryan to John Ward, 418 acres (DE/70) Lot 6

16 JUL 1844 George Grimes to John Bell, 125 acres - part of Grimes league adjacent to northwest tract now owned by Northcross, witnessede by A.M. Logan, J. Bell, M. Terry and John Atkinson.

5 MAY 1843 Wm. Mills of Montgomery County binds self to Micajah Terry for land on West fork of Mill Creek in Lot 3.

9 NOV 1845 John F. Barnett to Mickaj Terry, Lot 3 Western Division.

21 DEC 1848 George Grimes to Elias Elliot, 252 acres.

7 FEB 1847 Guy M. Bryan to Mikajah Terry Lot 2 (Western Division) on west fork of Mill Creek at 574 acres.

21 DEC 1850 Sam Kuykendall to John Manley, now of Walker Co, TX, 525 acres on forks of Mill Creek (Rest of Lot 3, Western Division)

9 SEP 1839 (B/333) Wm. J. Scott, 435 acres to Alfred Minton public auction 434 acres on Mill Creek from corner of Lot 8 N47W 950 vrs to a spring branch flowing S at 1000 vrs to Eaton's SW corner then S43W 440 v. to Spring Branch, then S to east bank of west fork, then down creek to upper corner of Lot 8 then with line of lot 8 242 v. to place of beginning. (Lot 9) Later Minton sold 211 acres September, 1851 in (DE/451) to John P. Shelborne (west ½ of Lot 9).

4 JUL 1838 Perry to John P. Shelburne (A/246) 921 acres - tract 10 on east side of west prong of Mill Creek beginning at Eaton's SW corner, with Eaton's line N43 1200 vrs to corner of Mrs. Kuykendall, thence N47 1200 vrs to back line of Mrs. Kuykendall, thence S43W 4900 vrs to East Bank of West Prong of Mill Creek, thence down creek to upper corner of Tract 9 thence with line of tract 9 2480 vrs to beginning.

25 DEC 1844 (C/19) John P. Jones to John P. Shelborn, Lot 11, 1198 acres for $1358, bounded on North by Mrs. Kuykendall, west by Carothers, South by West Fork, east by J.P. Shelborn).

18 APR 1851 (DE/449) Wm. Hill to J.P. Shelborn 11-1200 acres, Lot 11 Western Div. adjoining Carothers and Shelborn.

George Grimes League - Early Land Transactions

The following excerpts from land transactions in the George Grimes League in Austin, County, Texas, were made available by the Bellville Abstract Company to the author in 1992. The column "Record" indicates (Volume / Page) in the Deed Records of Austin County.

Date - Record	**Seller**	**Buyer**	**Description**
16 Mar 1831 Spanish "A" p. 105	Mexican Government	George Grimes	1 league on right margin of Mill Creek.
9 Jun 1831	George Grimes	Elisha Roberts	1 league on right margin of Mill Creek
18 Jun 1834 Spanish "G" #15	George Grimes	Elisha Roberts	1/2 league on Mill Creek
13 Aug 1839 (B/63)	George Grimes	Frederick Grimes	SE corner of league on Mill Creek.
6 Oct 1840 (B/145)	Harris Catlin, Sheriff for George Grimes, Sr.	T. Pillsbury, H.N. Cleveland for R. Kleberg	100 acres
26 Nov 1840 (B/159)	Robert Kleberg	David Ayres	100 acres
1 Jan 1841 (B/212)	David Ayers	D. Heddon, S. Day, A. Ayers	100 acres
4 Jan 1842 (B/295)	J. Harris Catlin Sheriff	Allen Norcross	100 acres
7 Oct 1844 (B/518)	Geo. Grimes	John Bell	125 acres
7 Dec 1858 (B/213)	F.P. Elliott	J.N. David	180 acres - on Long Branch in southern part of league next to Norcross.
21 Feb 1845 (C/25)	F. Grimes	Frederick Jordan	1 labor of land
13 Jun 1846 (C/132)	F. Jourden	A. K. Bellamen	177.5 acres on Mill Creek, east boundary line of Grimes league.
7 Apr 1848 (C/298)	G. Grimes	A.J. Grimes	185 acres
26 Dec 1848 (C/391)	G. Grimes	E. Elliott	252 acres
21 Feb 1849 (DE/10)	G. Grimes	W.E.K. Bellman	92 acres
20 Oct 1849 (DE/56)	J.T. Bell	E. Elliott	125 acres
1 Apr 1851 (F/149)	N. W. Bush, admin.	Elias Elliott	165 acres, Lot #4, survey by Charles Amthor on 10/11 March 1851

1 Apr 1851 (DE/349) Estate.	N.W. Bush, administrator Wm. Frampton Geo. Grimes Estate		108 acres at upper (NW) corner of #2 on Mill Creek and Lot 3, Grimes
1 Apr 1851 (DE/351)	N.W. Bush	Thos. Bell	125.5 acres (Lot #2, Grimes Estate)
1 Apr 1851 (DE/ 353)	N.W. Bush	A. McMillan	121 acres by SW corner Lot #5
15 Aug 1851 (DE/401)	N.W. Bush	A.J. Grimes	183 acres on Mill Creek in lower corner
15 Aug 1851 (F429)	B.S. Harrison	N.W. Bush	1/2 undivided interesat in 103 acres Lot #1
14 Jul 1851 (DE /426)	Wm. Frampton	B.L. Harrison	108 acres
9 Aug 1851 (DE/428)	E.A. & A.J. Grimes	B.L. Harrison	183 acres on Mill Creek
7 Jan 1852 (DE/563)	Thos. Bell	B.L. Harrison	125.5 acres , upper NW corner on Mill Creek
19 Aug 1851 (F/67)	E.A.K. Bellaman	Jonah C. Meek	92 acres
13 JAn 1853 (F/142)	James Jackson, admin. estate of Wm. Bellamen	Nathan W. Bush	92 acres
(F/251)	to public		1 acre for cemetery
17 Mar 1853 (F/281)	Elias Elliott	John Manley, Jas Meek & James A. Thompson	2 acres
1852 (F/425)	A. McMillan	John Manley	121 acres
17 Apr 1854 (F/510)	N.W. Bush	Elias Elliott	Meek tract adjoining Elliott homeplace on south and Manley on west
17 Apr 1854 (F/522)	Elias & Frances Elliott	James H. Meek	267 acres on Mill Creek
28 Jan 1854 (F/565)	B.S. & Lucinda Harrison	Logan Howard	233.5 acres + 125.5 acres + 103 acres
1 Nov 1854 (F/735)	J.P. & Margaret Renfroe	Edward Daughtry	795 ac., part of Elisha Roberts half league
27 Jan 1855 (IJ/38)	J.H. & H. Meek	J. Bonner	257 acres on south bank. Long Branch
20 Mar 1855 (IJ/161)	E. Elliott	F.J. Elliott	120 acres less 2 acres for school
2 Apr 1855 (IJ/92)	E. Elliott	E.E. Williamson	30 acres
4 Jil 1856 (IJ/506)	L.M. Howard	J.N. Daniel & J. Manley	233.5 acres
30 Dec 1856 (G/44)	Robt. Alexander	Rufus E. Campbell	all land he purchased from D.T. Ayres
15 Oct 1857 (G/225)	Ruffin Ward	E.C. Williams	30 acres + 87 acres
24 Oct 1857 (H/168)	Wm D&Elisabeth Woods	Farroll Shumake	108 acres - Lot #3
16 Nov 1858 (G/563)	Ben Harrison	N.W. Bush	183 acres

16 Dec 1858 (G/604)	Elinor (via Allen) Norcross	William Bonner	100 acres adj.residence of Jordan Bonner
23 Dec 1858 (H/170)	Farrell & Sarah Shumake	SIlas G. Howard	108 acres Lot #3
28 Dec 1858 (H/371)	John J. Jackson, admin	John Atkinson	6.5 acres on Long Branch
17 Jan 1859 (H/360)	N.W. Bush	J.A. Clemmons	183 acres
7 May 1859 (H/321)	J.J. Jackson, admin . estate of Wm. Bellaman	N. Holland & Z. Hunt	177.5 acres less 5 acres off SW corner (neighborhood schoolhouse)
30 May 1859 (H/360)	H. Holland & Z. Hunt	public for schoolhouse	5 acres
31 Oct 1859 (H/527)	J.J. Jackson, admin.	John Atkinson	6.5 acres

EARLY LOT AND NEARBY LAND SALES IN THE TOWN OF NELSONVILLE

18 Sep 1867 (M/704)	David D. & Sarah E. Nelson	J.S. Cole	1.5 acres on south side, Industry to Bellville public road.
20 Jun 1867 (M/705)	Nelson's	E.C. Williamson	1 acre, north side public road
18 Sep 1867 (M/706)	Nelson's	R.C. Burns	7200 sq. ft., north side public road
18 Sep 1867 (M/707)	Nelson's	Ann D. Lott	1 acre
11 Nov 1867 (M/734)	Nelson's	P.L. Gendrean,George Meyer	7200 sq. ft. N. side road, Lot #!, Block #3
4 Dec 1867 (N/41)	J.W. Bethany	Lewis, Flake & Bethany	1 acre – dwelling of Dr. J..S. Cole
14 Dec 1867 (N/41)	J.W. Bethany	Lewis, Flake & Bethany	all of 1/2 interest in lot in Nelsonville on which stands store of Lewis, Flake & Bethany and room of G.W. Foster Lodge.
14 Dec 1867 (N/42)	J.W. Bethany	G.W. Foster Lodge	all of 1/2 interest in lot of store & lodge
31 Jan 1868 (N/19)	Nelson's	Isaac Lewis	14,400 sq. ft. (lots 3&4) in Block #2
31 Jan 1868 (N/20)	Nelson's	Edward Brune	2 acres
31 Jan 1868 (O/130)	Nelson's	J. W. Kersh	1 acre
6 Mar 1868 (N/79)	Nelson's	S.D. Flake	7200 sq. ft. Lot #4 Block #5
6 Mar 1868 (N/89)	Nelson's	Gustav Prause	1 acre
26 Mar 1868 (N/77)	Nelson's	J. H. McMillian	7200 sq. ft. Lot #2 Block #2
26 Mar 1868 (N/78)	J.A. McMillian	Isaac Lewis	Lot #2 Block #2
26 Mar 1868 (N/153)	Nelson's	Wm. Barnhill	7200 sq. ft. Lot #5 Block #5
26 Mar 11868 (N/204)	Nelson's	P.L. Gendrean	1 acre
19 May 1868 (N/240)	Nelson's	Gottlieb Hilboldt	7200 sq. ft.
14 Jul 1869 (O/49)	S.D. Flake	I. Lewis & J.W. Bethany	
30 Jul 1869 (O/45)	Nelson's	J.S. Cole	1.2 acres
30 Jul 1869 (O/46)	Nelson's	J.W. Bethany, J. Manley, J.S. Cole	Lot # @: 14.400 sq ft, #1 1 5/8 acres, No. 3: W.Z. Dixon, J.H. Bradbury

845 sq ft. (School and church) Elias Elliott, W.A. Thompson
W.L. Shelburn, Wm. Thompson

2 Mar 1870 (O/490)	John Manley	J. Ward	2 acres
14 Apr 1870 (O/510)	Bethany & Lewis	P.S. Chessher	750 sq varas
30 Apr 1870 (O/524)	Bethany	F. Moore	12,320 sq. varas
23 May 1870 (O/625)	J.&E. A. Ward	S. Howard	7.4 acres
21 Jan 1867 (N/467)	Joseph & Verna Malyna	D. Heitmann	80 acres + 320 acres
21 Jan 1867 (N/469)	Joseph & Anna Kantor	D. Heitmann	100 acres
21 Jan 1867 (N/470)	Steven & Anna Gabriss	D. Heitmann	100 acres - part of Roberts division
19 Nov 1868 (N/401)	Campbell	George Meyer	177.5 acres
20 Nov 1868 (N/413)	CN, MA Quillen,E. Elliott	John A. Campbell	33 acres
21 Jun 1869 (O/282)	J.W. Bethany	N. Brune	15 acres
30 Sep 1869 ()/114)G.&M.	Meyer	J.W. Bouldin	84 5/8 acres
5 Jan 1870 (O/280)	Nelson's	Isaac Lewis	12.5 acres
31 Jan 1870 (O/279)	Nelson's	E.C. Williamson	23 acres

Appendix II: Cemetery Records

APPENDIX I

Cemetery Records

The following pages are records of all cemeteries located in the lower forks of Mill Creek, as reproduced from the book "The Cemeteries of Austin County, Texas". One area cemetery, Garnett/Bonner near Oak Hill, was not included in the original published version of the book. The data from this cemetery was recorded by the author.

BETHANY CEMETERY

Location of Bethany cemetery: Located west of Nelsonville on Hwy 159 Aproximately 1\2 mile.

Bethany, E.A.
5 January 1875
4 August 1878

Ogg, Walter
11 November 1829
1 June 1881

Bell, A. J.
4 August 1818
9 June 1885

Bell infant
25 May 1873
3 June 1885

Bethany, Thomas A.
1864
22 January 1864

Infant son of
E.C. and S.E.
15 July 1885
17 August 1886

Bethany infant
17 September 1879
4 June 1881

Bethany, James W.
4 April 1824
10 June 1889

Flake, Stubin O.
No date given
15 December 1879

Flake, Mary
No date given
4 January 1965

Minton infant
30 October 1875
18 November 1875

Bethany infant
17 November 1881
11 April 1884

Bethany, Thomas
16 February 1777
6 April 1869

Tison, Adrianna C.
10 October 1828
1 July 1880

Unmarked grave
Unmarked grave
Unmarked grave
Unmarked grave

BOULDIN (FLAKE) CEMETERY

Location of (Flake) Bouldin cemetery: From Bellville, take 159 West to Nelsonville. In Nelsonville, before 2502, turn left on Skalak Road. The Suen Cemetery is to the left, but this cemetery is to the right. About 1\10 mile on Tieman Road you make a 90 turn. After this turn, continue about 3\10 mile. Cemetery is on right in brush and trees. You can not see cemetery from the road. This is private property.

Flake, Garfield
13 March 1885
8 December 1968

Flake, Pearle M.
17 January 1888
18 August 1956

Flake, Delaney
2 April 1918
9 July 1956

Banks, Annie
29 August 1870
21 June 1948

Unmarked grave
Unmarked grave

Bouldin, Susie
1 September 1874
19 March 1916

4 unmarked graves

Bouldin, Nadine
1 March 1900
18 August 1926

Flake, Johann
March 1843
5 July 1909

Keener, Mattie
9 April 1875
15 July 1952

Glinger, Jairet
9 September 1859
8 October 1906

BURNS CEMETERY

Location of Burns cemetery: Go north on Hwy 36 and turn left off of FM 159. Go west to Oak Hill and turn south on Sycamore Crossing and when you come to Macat Ranch #2 entrance; enter, the cemetery is on your right past the barn.

Burns, R.C.
No date given
31 March 1874

Burns, Ehughson
28 December 1876
25 September 1880

DIXON-GRIMES CEMETERY

Location of Dixon-Grimes Family cemetery: It is located on the Haedge farm, northwest of Nelsonville.

Williamson, E.C. 14 November 1833 16 July 1881	Dixon, Rebecca 10 November 1813 10 May 1878	Beathe, Karl 8 October 1868 18 October 1906
Williamson, Annie S. 10 July 1855 18 June 1882	Dekalb, John 31 October 1846 14 January 1878	Beathe, William Born and Died 1901
Edgar, Millie 1 January 1872 19 August 1877	Barnett, Tabbie May 30 June 1873 10 December 1880	Baby Lewis No dates given
Dixon, William Z. 22 February 1823 10 May 1878	Dixon, Dr. J.D. 31 October 1846 14 January 1873	Baby Harvel No dates given

FLAKE'S CEMETERIES (see also BOULDIN - FLAKE)

Location of Flake's cemeteries: There are two cemeteries. From New Ulm, go east on 1094 for 4 miles. Turn left on New Bremen road of 3.2 miles to intersection. Turn left at intersection and go 1.6 miles. Turn right at T and .1 mile to corner. It is right off the corner.

Robertson, Allen 18 June 1865 25 August 1953	Davis, W.T. 14 March 1863 18 June 1936	Robertson, Nancy 25 December 1875 7 July 1940
Ray, Elma A. 1909 1984	Davis, Mary 18 August 1860 No date given	Flakes, Mary 27 July 1891 9 March 1922
		Unmarked grave Unmarked grave

The location of the other Flake cemetery: Burials are on V.H. Ueckert place approximately 5 miles west of Bellville on State Hwy 159 and approximately 300 feet south of Highway.

Wilson, I.N. 15 June 1838 25 March 1875	Daniel, Laura J. 13 October 1868 4 July 1882	Flake, Thomas M. No date given 5 May 1862
Hasty, Mrs. A. 5 December 1844 27 April 1865	Lee, A.J. 17 October 1813 27 January 1892	Unmarked grave Unmarked grave

I-3

Garnett/Bonner - an early and still active black cemetery in Oak Hill near Sycamore Crossing Road, consists of two neighboring plots, apparently primarily for the Garnett and Bonner families.

East Plot - Bonner: 7 known interrments, one marked.

Mrs. Kate Bonner	12 AUG 1880	1 NOV 1979

West Plot - Garnett: 20 known interrments, 10 marked

Vinie Garnett	5 JUL 1825	18 JUL 1920
Mrs. Ora Armstrong	1888	1986
George Fletcher	7 JAN 1889	30 AUG 1952
Chester Garnett	1892	1974
Robert Garnett, Jr	1895	1985
Mrs. Emaline Spates	1900	1990
Maryan Garnett	10 JUL 1907	7 OCT 1915
Eddie Garnett	12 MAR 1915	2 APR 1915
Robert Garnett, Sr.		5 JAN 1941
Eliza Garnett		21 JUL 1953

HAEDGE FAMILY PLOT

Location of Haedge Family cemetery: It is north of Nelsonville off of F.M. 2502.

Haedge, Bertha
13 October 1887
8 October 1985

Haedge, Mary
8 October 1846
2 February 1919

Haedge, Otto
28 September 1870
16 November 1936

Haedge, Charles
18 January 1837
10 August 1913

Unmarked grave
Unmarked grave
Unmarked grave

Unmarked grave
Unmarked grave

JOCHEC CEMETERY

Location of Jochec cemetery: It is located on Tieman road in Nelsonville.

Jochec, Karolina
13 March 1833
3 November 1923

Jochec, George
No date given
18 March 1883

Jochec, Karolina J
No date given

Jochec, Charles
21 November 1878
28 January 1913

Jochec, Lennard
1 September 1936
8 February 1938

Unknown grave

I-4

NATIONAL CEMETERY

Location of National cemetery: Take Hwy 159 west out of Bellville. Go thru Nelsonville to 1754. Turn right and cemetery will be on the left about 2 / 10 mile.

Macat, Ernest
14 May 1916
17 March 1985

Stepan, David Ray
28 February 1944
2 October 1983

Schovajsa, Emil H
9 August 1900
5 August 1981

Schovajsa, Albina
25 December 1900
24 November 1984

Mikeska, Harry J
17 December 1911
19 Novemer 1981

Dean, Douglas C
12 July 1928
10 July 1982

Schovajsa, Willie
25 March 1909
24 April 1983

Zettle, Alfred
20 March 1910
29 February 1980

Schovajsa, Olga
11 February 1905
18 January 1980

Chernosky, Otto
No date given
27 July 1985

Ueckert, Alfred
13 September 1911
19 April 1983

Richard, Leopold
8 March 1900
22 September 1980

Richard, Fannie
23 April 1904
20 November 1984

Kamas, Edwin
9 April 1928
21 February 1983

Surovik, Frank
1 April 1917
12 November 1982

Surovik, Esther
13 January 1919
5 September 1979

Krizan, Frank
6 November 1903
9 February 1979

Krizan, Hermina
8 September 1906
No date given

Sisa, John
14 February 1899
12 September 1982

Sisa, Olga
16 March 1903
19 September 1988

Mikeska, Otto
17 April 1944
4 March 1981

Mikeska, Otta
8 July 1918
6 January 1978

Mikeska, Joseph
15 June 1905
No date given

Mikeska, Tillie
1 October 1904
16 July 1978

Jurik, Annie R
19 May 1931
19 June 1931

Taska, Lonnie Dee
1930
1933

Stephan, John A
21 March 1932
28 July 1933

Sisa, Gardina A
27 July 1933
2 October 1933

Schovajsa, Leroy
31 May 1935
1 June 1935

Unmarked grave

Macat, Erwin S
5 July 1935
16 June 1936

I-5

Taska, Ellis
21 March 1932
6 May 1978

Slacik, Willie
5 May 1910
11 February 1979

Maresh, Wilma
3 January 1918
13 January 1977

Broughton, Rosalie
23 July 1900
28 February 1982

Macat, Otto
15 November 1925
17 December 1979

Schramm, Michael
14 March 1966
2 December 1981

Schramm, Mike A
14 March 1966
16 December 1979

Sloupensky, Jan
14 March 1843
1895

Sloupensky, Anna
26 December 1847
17 February 1925

Mikeska, Frane
15 December 1831
14 April 1896

Mikeska, Rozara
1 May 1835
16 November 1908

Maresh, Ed
31 August 1906
No date given

Maresh, Annie
24 February 1914
5 March 1975

Stephan, John A
29 January 1904
13 September 1975

Stephan, William M
4 October 1898
14 April 1982

Kamas, William
25 November 1893
10 August 1982

Kamas, Lillie
21 August 1893
14 August 1979

Smilek, Paul
25 September 1903
29 December 1975

Schroeder, David G
23 March 1940
21 September 1981

Jochec, Louis
16 June 1898
7 August 1978

Chernosky, Norris
6 December 1929
29 May 1977

Krause, Emma S
17 July 1911
14 October 1984

Shupak, Jesse F
14 October 1906
3 February 1981

Syptak, Jonathon
9 September 1982
9 September 1982

Syptak, Joseph
21 January 1982
21 January 1982

Mikeska, Matthew
22 July 1981
22 July 1981

Unmarked grave

Taska, Geo.
1871
1908

Unmarked grave

Pomykal, Joe
1904
1980

Pomykal, Vlasta
1904
No date given

Duebbe, Adolph
24 July 1919
22 June 1981

Masar, Joe
19 January 1931
23 July 1975

Stasny, Edmund A
2 August 1891
19 June 1975

Stasny, Marie
23 December 1893
22 February 1972

Surovik, Walter
No date given
23 July 1985

Siptak, Edwin
24 May 1907
20 October 1973

Siptak, Minnie
21 February 1909
25 July 1979

Mikeska, Jerry D
14 August 1899
12 October 1973

Holba, John
5 October 1897
24 November 1972

Holba, Louisa
24 September 1902
23 August 1977

Kamas, Mary R
1 September 1876
28 October 1972

Barnett, Joseph E
3 April 1909
No date given

I-6

Sisa, Annie
1 August 1891
26 June 1979

Renner, Alford
3 October 1907
16 May 1985

Barnett, Annie V
3 September 1903
27 December 1970

Maresh, Otto J
16 July 1912
10 February 1970

Maresh, Lula B
4 October 1909
No date given

Lubojasky, Frank
18 December 1893
4 December 1969

Lubojasky, Annie
10 December 1898
9 November 1980

Beckmann, Edwin
4 September 1902
23 June 1966

Beckmann, Ladella
7 September 1902
1987

Mikeska, Marian
20 November 1900
22 June 1968

Schiller, Bohuslav
23 November 1894
27 February 1985

Schiller, Alma
11 May 1894
30 March 1972

Grebe, Sidney
25 October 1949
15 January 1975

Kudlacek, Rudolph
31 July 1908
15 October 1970

Schroeder, Edna
29 November 1921
12 January 1970

Stalmach, Edwin
6 December 1896
11 July 1984

Stalmach, Lydia
20 September 1909
18 March 1983

Mikeska, John
10 November 1907
31 October 1968

Mikeska, Milada O
28 August 1908
No date given

Taska, Frank
19 April 1895
28 January 1969

Taska, Frances
22 November 1898
No date given

Chaloupka, Vince B
5 March 1913
28 April 1965

Chaloupka, Maxine
20 June 1917
No date given

Kamas, John P
6 March 1890
24 May 1964

Kamas, Hermina A
31 December 1897
2 April 1974

Grebe, Reuben J
No date given
24 October 1975

Shupak, Willie
17 August 1883
21 May 1965

Shupak, Annie
28 May 1882
22 January 1966

Chernosky, Milady
20 June 1903
30 March 1979

Mehner, Ernst
16 June 1890
18 November 1968

Mehner, Hertha
22 September 1892
4 Janaury 1970

McKinney, Olga A
17 July 1911
No date given

McKinney, Mollie
24 September 1919
19 September 1975

Janecek, Lydia
16 September 1891
2 May 1979

Susen, Willie
9 December 1891
29 May 1972

Susen, Herminia
28 September 1914
3 June 1980

Kamas, Frances
3 March 1867
13 August 1958

Jurik, Anna
15 May 1895
6 October 1958

Jurik, John L
29 December 1892
12 February 1959

Mikeska, Anton
5 September 1907
25 September 1959

Mikeska, Ella
22 August 1908
No date given

Jurik, Joe
7 April 1889
10 November 1959

I-7

Maresh, Alvin
9 July 1901
28 June 1968

Schmalriede, Fred
9 August 1889
4 November 1977

Schmalriede, Helena
21 July 1887
13 February 1961

Liska, Louise
28 November 1876
21 November 1961

Liska, Will
15 May 1896
4 December 1962

Liska, Frank
20 Janaury 1898
3 Janaury 1977

Slovak, Joseph
26 August 1880
20 December 1961

Slovak, Theresie
27 February 1884
29 November 1972

Zettel, Charlie J
11 July 1917
8 April 1962

Sefcik, Joseph
22 December 1876
16 January 1963

Sefcik, Mary
6 January 1878
9 October 1962

Ripple, Henry C
19 July 1903
1 June 1974

Chaloupka, Ladislav
24 March 1909
4 June 1975

Chaloupka, Theresa
28 January 1912
No date given

Mikeska, Thomas
24 February 1899
9 July 1961

Mikeska, Mary
6 September 1901
No date given

Meinke, Paul A
11 May 1903
7 October 1961

Meinke, Vlasta
11 September 1909
No date given

Chernosky, Paula J
12 April 1960
19 January 1962

Siptak, Delmo
1 January 1925
25 June 1963

Blackwell, Mildred
24 December 1924
19 April 1965

Coufal, Joseph F
8 September 1886
7 August 1975

Coufal, Anna O
30 July 1890
14 April 1982

Siptak, Charlie
1 June 1888
30 August 1971

Siptak, Annie
17 March 1891
3 March 1968

Maresh, Alfred E
8 October 1915
22 June 1979

Maresh, Olga A
12 March 1919
20 September 1977

Shupak, Larry W
14 December 1957
20 December 1957

Schovajsa, Sadie F
16 March 1916
8 January 1958

Fick, Willie
14 December 1915
9 May 1954

Liska, John
8 January 1894
13 July 1954

Liska, Minnie
26 August 1904
No date given

Schimara, Calvin W
17 June 1948
1 December 1959

Uhrik, Frank
18 March 1882
19 January 1955

Uhrik, Fannie
1 January 1884
3 January 1976

Stephan, Alfred
1902
1955

Stephan, Ruth O
1905
30 January 1985

Stephan, Otto H
2 June 1906
23 May 1981

Stephan, Earnest
13 July 1919
13 March 1957

Chernosky, Ignac
27 November 1871
29 April 1957

Chernosky, Cecelia
26 October 1885
18 August 1969

Reed, Lydia
1899
1957

I-8

Reed, Frank Bell
1905
1960

Zettel, Lillie M
11 December 1910
6 October 1957

Zettel, Willie E
17 October 1912
6 November 1979

Tylajka, Steven
25 August 1887
30 January 1959

Zettel, Donna Jo
Born and Died
13 November 1960

Baby unknown
1984

Mikeska, John M
14 March 1968
15 March 1968

Krause, Keith A
Born and died
22 December 1971

Maresh, Willie
No date given
30 September 1985

Chaloupka, Vincenc
3 April 1888
2 August 1963

Chaloupka, Albina
27 October 1888
24 March 1954

Baletka, Marie
1871
1953

Masar, Edwin
5 April 1936
20 April 1953

Masar, Joe
7 April 1904
6 October 1969

Masar, Emlie
25 June 1906
No date given

Drevojanek, Mathilda
16 February 1898
12 March 1952

Drevojanek, Wilhelm
29 August 1887
21 April 1959

Krause, Dennis E
4 January 1933
6 November 1951

Krause, Elsie O
25 January 1910
No date given

Krause, Edwin
12 October 1907
No date given

Sebesta, Frank
2 February 1873
13 February 1951

Sebesta, Albina
15 September 1887
19 December 1965

Sebesta, Joseph
9 March 1870
15 July 1949

Sebesta, Anna
21 February 1879
12 November 1961

Bravenec, Otto
17 October 1908
No date given

Bravenec, Lydia
23 December 1908
No date given

Bravenec, Mary
4 August 1869
22 January 1949

Bravenec, Tom
18 May 1873
7 March 1952

Maresh, Edwin
3 February 1900
9 July 1965

Chaka, Jerry H
1910
1948

Sisa, Joe
18 August 1889
13 November 1967

Sisa, Albina
15 August 1892
26 June 1963

Sisa, Isidor A
5 January 1918
8 April 1948

Surovik, Frantiska
6 January 1873
11 December 1943

Surovik, Tomas
27 November 1867
29 January 1947

Siptak, John
15 February 1877
12 September 1954

Siptak, Francis
20 March 1882
25 August 1939

Maresh, Joseph
28 September 1874
13 October 1937

Maresh, Agnes
14 May 1878
5 January 1959

Stalmach, John
23 March 1861
1 February 1940

Stalmach, Theresia
7 April 1864
30 September 1937

Krause, Herman
11 November 1883
2 February 1940

I-9

Krause, Anna
24 October 1883
12 April 1979

Balusek, John
8 June 1879
12 October 1940

Hasting, John W
17 October 1885
25 February 1942

Hasting, Karoline B
21 September 1896
26 May 1956

Balusek, Rose
14 March 1890
21 December 1975

Kamas, Mary
1872
1941

Esterak, Frantiska
28 December 1865
16 February 1942

Esterak, Jan
27 March 1868
7 January 1944

Esterak, Vincencie
24 December 1871
29 May 1944

Esterak, Rozalie
16 March 1875
6 February 1958

Plasek, Teresa
14 February 1870
26 June 1944

Plasek, Frank
20 June 1866
28 September 1956

Koppa, Joe
1 May 1864
14 April 1945

Koppa, Anna
10 May 1867
14 July 1950

Mikeska, Thomas
2 January 1880
9 January 1946

Mikeska, Anna
9 February 1881
24 July 1962

Zettel, Anna
7 February 1888
17 June 1946

Zettel, John
6 March 1884
7 October 1966

Krause, Paul
1898
1946

Krause, Hattie
1896
1980

Maresh, Willie E
3 Janaury 1893
19 June 1951

Maresh, Frank B
15 November 1895
16 April 1968

Stalbaum, Mary
19 August 1877
4 April 1962

Stalbaum, William
4 January 1873
5 August 1952

Seda, Annie
7 July 1872
8 November 1949

Unmarked grave

Janecek, Vilem
3 November 1861
7 March 1940

Janecek, Terezie
24 June 1867
22 December 1942

Siptak, Joe
17 July 1875
8 January 1940

Siptak, Minnie
13 November 1877
6 November 1954

Mares, Vincence
4 December 1864
28 June 1939

Unmarked grave

Surovik, Rosie
1 November 1876
29 May 1937

Surovik, Jan
3 April 1872
23 March 1942

Kamas, Jimmie
1937
1939

Kamas, Theresa
13 March 1849
27 August 1936

Kamas, Thomas
24 December 1845
9 April 1939

Gerhart, Rozalie
March 1859
18 August 1936

Unmarked grave

Maresh, Annie
4 April 1877
16 December 1935

Maresh, Frank B
10 November 1870
5 January 1948

Sebesta, Edmund E
20 April 1915
14 October 1946

Stalmach, Edmund F
6 December 1896
15 May 1946

I-10

Maresh, Edwin Jr.
4 January 1931
27 June 1935

Holba, Josef
28 January 1855
18 October 1947

Holba, Frantiska
28 February 1859
23 January 1935

Kamas, J.C.
10 February 1876
17 November 1934

Sebesta, Anna
6 December 1884
7 September 1939

Sebesta, Karel
25 February 1878
4 June 1933

Mikeska, John F
1874
1947

Mikeska, Theresa M
1875
1956

Sebesta, Raymond
16 May 1921
16 April 1947

Lancer, Jos
14 March 1868
8 January 1891

Uherka, Katerina
12 March 1820
24 January 1897

Uherka, Jan
26 June 1816
26 January 1891

Kamaz, Jan
16 December 1839
8 October 1891

Cernocka, Josefa
8 February 1872
20 January 1899

Kamas, Anna
28 September 1832
2 February 1915

Kamas, Thomas
12 December 1840
10 February 1900

Kroulik, Theresa
9 September 1875
13 September 1900

Bravanec, Jan
3 March 1842
10 October 1900

Bravanec, Anna
28 May 1851
19 September 1936

Muery, Henriette
30 August 1836
8 June 1901

Unmarked grave

Wernli, Jacob
11 March 1874
26 November 1874

Unmarked grave

Wernli, Jacob
3 August 1865
14 July 1905

Manzel, Josef
15 July 1859
18 December 1932

Manzelka, Marie
3 July 1861
24 April 1938

Schimara, Frances
21 December 1862
16 August 1934

Schimara, Joseph
3 April 1857
27 August 1940

Slacik, John
1866
1945

Slacik, Mary
1871
1952

Slacik, Lydie F
1898
1946

Balusek, Frank
7 March 1850
19 March 1935

Balusek, Anna
20 October 1852
31 Janaury 1944

Sisa, Frantisek
7 October 1865
13 February 1925

Sisa, Rosalie
14 October 1861
11 June 1929

Kamas, Anna
10 February 1844
27 ? 1925

Sefcek, Jan
No date given
21 November 1925

Sefcek, Frantiska
No date given
20 January 1948

Shupak, John R
3 October 1893
26 January 1927

Shupak, Mary T
4 April 1894
3 December 1980

Bravenec, Louise
10 October 1879
26 February 1927

Bravenec, John J
2 March 1860
27 June 1943

Schupak, Frank
24 October 1889
6 April 1927

I-11

Schupak, Mary
26 August 1894
17 January 1971

Bravenec, Anna
18 December 1862
27 October 1927

Bravenec, Jan
25 June 1866
23 November 1936

Sebesta, Frantiska
8 October 1867
9 February 1928

Coufal, Frances
1840
1928

Bartay, Henry
7 January 1868
21 January 1944

Bartay, Isabell
29 March 1875
24 October 1964

Schimara, Willie
28 December 1894
7 June 1929

Macat, Frank
6 March 1895
7 February 1930

Macat, Albina
5 November 1896
30 January 1981

Macat, Joseph
15 May 1855
31 January 1932

Macat, Terezie
16 March 1854
3 December 1949

Elsik, John
8 January 1857
12 December 1930

Elsik, Francie
25 March 1866
27 August 1932

Unmarked grave

Drevojanek, Josef
29 August 1885
14 August 1930

Mares, Henry J
11 February 1891
3 May 1924

Andreas, Hermann
1865
1923

Andreas, Minnie
1869
1953

Sisa, Veronyka
16 October 1847
1923

Kudlacek, John
11 November 1867
9 December 1953

Kudlacek, Albina
1 January 1885
4 December 1975

Slacikova, Anna
28 March 1835
1 March 1889

Slacikova, Josef
4 December 1836
28 May 1923

Unmarked grave

Sailer, Marie
29 September 1861
17 June 1909

Sailer, August
12 May 1858
26 August 1932

Glaser, Fredeick W
27 November 1826
6 July 1910

Esterak, Rozalie
14 February 1833
7 November 1911

Esterak, Josef
29 January 1832
24 December 1914

Kamas, Anna
17 July 1869
23 August 1918

Kamas, Josef
6 October 1857
7 February 1929

Kamas, Rozina
27 May 1858
19 May 1945

Sebesta, Anna
2 February 1835
28 April 1920

Minton, Teresie
5 June 1880
August 1921

Minton, John
23 March 1875
7 July 1962

Krause, Herma
9 April 1922
No date given

Krause, Theresa
18 December 1936
1 November 1959

Stepan, Josef
19 March 1858
31 May 1922

Stephan, Anna
December 1861
2 January 1932

Drevojanek, Thomas
7 August 1883
13 October 1922

Surovik, Frank
No date given
30 June 1937

Kudlacek, Lydia
5 January 1904
31 August 1919

I-12

Kudlacek, Annie
11 March 1902
19 February 1920

Siller, Anna
6 March 1860
27 September 1923

Siller, Joseph
8 May 1857
1 February 1938

4 Unmarked grave

Baletka, John
7 October 1870
11 April 1933

Roesler, Elba
No date given
16 February 1984

Roesler, Eleonora
5 February 1875
15 January 1944

Roesler, Robert
3 August 1878
12 February 1974

Roesler, Leon
28 January 1910
2 March 1918

Janek, Katerina
20 January 1873
12 October 1909

Schovajse, Olga
3 February 1903
24 April 1905

Janek, Katerina
20 February 1832
12 May 1913

Janek, Thomas
30 December 1815
17 October 1900

Janek, Tomas
18 December 1852
7 March 1927

Janek, Emma
1863
28 September 1888

Krause, Martin
10 August 1826
27 July 1885

Krause, Friedrich
20 July 1825
2 October 1882

Krause, Henriette
No dates given

31 Unmarked graves

Bravenec, Joseph
12 November 1889
3 November 1892

Bravenec, Martin
3 May 1880
16 July 1884

Maresova, Terezie
1902
No date given

Sefcik, Frantisek
23 September 1838
11 December 1902

Hanka, Anton Dr.
3 April 1813
30 April 1904

Susen, Charles
25 January 1889
5 August 1915

Susen, Anna
2 September 1892
14 August 1979

Schovajsa, Jan J
11 August 1893
28 April 1916

Schovjsa, Jan
22 March 1872
1 May 1938

Schovajsa, Frantiska
8 May 1869
1 December 1943

Jurchak, John
27 May 1862
24 May 1930

Taska, Elvis O
1925
1925

Taska, Gladys V
1924
1924

Taska, Irvin O
1921
1923

Shupak, Marie O
24 April 1921
13 March 1922

Simara, Stephan
26 March 1814
1898

Simara, Marie
26 August 1890
No date given

Kamaz, Jan
16 December 1839
8 October 1891

Rychlik, Johana
22 June 1872
23 October 1897

Unmarked grave
Unmarked grave

Plasek, Josef
11 February 1849
17 August 1899

Mares, Jan M
1830
2 September 1904

Mares, Anna
1832
10 February 1919

Siptak, Anna
5 February 1857
11 January 1937

I-13

Suptak, Rozalie
19 January 1885
18 May 1905

Mikeska, Frances
4 February 1879
13 May 1966

Mikeska, Joseph
9 December 1877
22 August 1905

Mikeska, Anna
16 January 1859
24 July 1937

Susen, Rozalie
25 March 1882
1908

Susen, Frantisek
21 October 1883
26 July 1910

Schovajsa, Frantiska
12 November 1901
9 September 1917

Schovajsa, Frank
28 November 1880
13 January 1963

Schovajsa, Frances
6 January 1881
27 July 1970

Fraktiser, Lesni
16 July 1873
22 January 1889

Susen, Terzie
30 October 1898
21 October 1918

Susen, Rozalie
27 August 1853
5 August 1934

Susen, Jan
1852
11 July 1945

Susen, Olga
2 February 1911
8 January 1925

Maresh, Frances
14 May 1878
17 January 1932

Maresh, Wilem
6 December 1870
28 January 1945

Esterak, Chas.
22 November 1859
6 April 1933

Jurck, Lonie
1920
30 January 1921

Unmarked grave
Unmarked grave

Krause, Noma
24 September 1921
No date given

Kamas, Frantisek
6 September 1900
6 September 1900

9 Unmarked graves

Zettel, Donna
Born and Died
6 November 1954

Sebesta, David
25 July 1952
26 July 1952

Milberger, D.F.
No date given
1945

Milberger, R.J.
No date given
1942

Maresh, Alfred Jr.
28 May 1939
5 July 1939

Maresh, Ben
26 June 1939
28 June 1939

Supak, Jan
6 August 1850
29 January 1901

Supak, Anna
27 September 1858
22 February 1932

Unmarked grave

3 Lindeman infants
No dates given

Siller, Karel
29 September 1815
10 July 1879

Siller, Ana
26 July 1822
26 May 1889

Lindeman infant
No dates given

Malechek, Alvina
23 July 1858
16 September 1902

Unmarked grave
Unmarked grave
Unmarked grave

Slacik, Katerina
30 April 1848
23 October 1925

14 Unmarked graves

Janecek, Monroe Josef
12 January 1918
28 January 1918

Unmarked grave
Unmarked grav

Taske, Frank
1927
1928

Bernshausen, Edna
12 March 1928
30 December 1928

Jochec, Wilborn
1 June 1930
1 June 1930

Jochec, Wilfred
1 June 1930
1 June 1930

I-14

SCRANTON GROVE CEMETERY

Location of Scranton Grove cemetery: Starting from the town of Bellville, go west on Hwy 159 and turn right on FM 2502. Go about 3 miles, then turn right onto Ueckert road. At the mailbox of John R. Mikeska, turn left on first road past mailbox. Pavement ends and the cemetery is on top of the hill.

Peters, Henry
3 February 1857
13 November 1930

Peters, Friedericke
2 May 1852
12 September 1929

Mikeska, Willie H
10 February 1905
17 June 1971

Blum, August Paul
30 April 1886
17 Janaury 1963

Ueckert, Willie C
29 November 1883
3 September 1947

Peters, Annie
5 November 1895
6 November 1934

Mikeska, Bertha L
12 September 1879
20 June 1957

Mikeska, John K
20 June 1867
19 August 1939

Ueckert, Adele G B
15 January 1829
6 March 1879

Ueckert, Richard
28 September 1847
5 March 1890

Ueckert daughter
1874
1877

Huff, Olivia
30 August 1904
21 June 1974

Huff, Richard
22 January 1872
15 February 1948

Huff, Frieda
7 September 1881
11 February 1949

Davis, William L
31 July 1905
7 November 1970

Leps, Henriette
4 August 1889
6 July 1895

Roesler, Ida
7 November 1850
5 April 1901

Roesler, August
23 January 1836
20 July 1933

Mikeska, Hilda
1898
1904

Mikeska, Edwin
1896
1896

Roesler, Martha
28 December 1873
7 October 1920

Roesler, Clara
29 April 1884
28 July 1970

Mikeska, Ferry
7 March 1905
6 October 1928

Ueckert, unknown
1813
1884

Uecket, Sophie
1870
1932

Ueckert, Otto
1877
1962

Mikeska, Frank W
31 March 1870
28 November 1953

Mikeska, Henrietta
24 June 1875
21 December 1968

Leps, Ede
13 October 1912
19 November 1912

Leps, Gottlieb
26 July 1839
27 April 1912

Leps, Gottlieb
1 August 1873
17 September 1936

Schmidt, Lora
2 August 1899
4 September 1899

Wunderling, Emma
19 March 1816
31 December 1911

Wunderling, Henrich
16 August 1843
9 January 1912

Ueckert, Clara A
6 February 1871
23 July 1875

Ueckert, Fritz W
5 October 1874
7 November 1875

Pochmann, Katharine
No dates given

Pochmann, Franz A
26 June 1795
8 January 1877

Hochbaum, Johan
15 April 1812
1875

Hochbaum, Friedericka
17 March 1816
1875

Kasse, Carl
6 September 1836
1 December 1879

Hartman, Andreas
7 December 1850
3 March 1913

SHELBURNE CEMETERY

Location of Shellburne cemetery: Take Hwy 159 west out of Nelsonville to Tieman road. Turn left and go approximately 1 mile to Zettel road. Turn right and go approximately 1 mile. Cemetery is on the left side of road.

Shelburne, William
24 January 1823
2 February 1878

James, Matti
4 September 1882
13 September 1882

Shelburne, Mary
2 July 1832
23 July 1893

Shelburne, J.P.
28 December 1790
5 November 1871

Shelburne, Nancy
20 September 1971
3 June 1858

Dunkin, Jane
20 September 1771
10 August 1851

Shellburne, Mary
29 March 1830
9 June 1845

Minton, John
No dates given

Minton, Jane
12 January 1816
6 April 1824

Minton, John
5 April 1852
1 February 1876

Minton, Alfred
No date given
26 October 1852

SUSEN CEMETERY

Location of Susen cemetery: Starting from the Town of Nelsonville, go south on Skalak road. Turn left; cemetery will be to the immediate right. There is a sign at the gate.

Siller, Jan
No date givne
19 July 1883

Siller, Rosalie
No date given
20 April 1897

Schiller,Sister Anna
1886
1907

Miller, Joachim
10 January 1849
13 July 1921

Miller, Amalie
10 December 1853
11 April 1891

Lesikar, Frantiska
1 March 1871
18 November 1952

Pavelek, Jan
27 December 1836
29 April 1898

Pavelek, Hedwig A
1841
22 February 1904

Pavelek, Jan
1866
14 February 1904
Kasparek, Anna
24 December 1911
11 January 1913

Golan, Amelia
No date given

Golan, Alvina
27 May 1880
18 April 1936

Pavelek, Joseph
17 February 1873
16 June 1905

Vacusek, Lydie
28 June 1898
21 July 1917

Vacusek, Annie
13 February 1882
21 December 1928

Vacusek, Frank
4 October 1872
12 January 1962

Walicek, Adolph
20 August 1870
5 March 1945

Walicek, Theresa
12 April 1876
10 September 1956

Mikeska, Veronica
26 November 1836
3 October 1907

Mikeska, Jiri
30 September 1837
4 March 1911

Mikeska, George Sr.
9 December 1864
26 June 1950

Mikeska, Anna
8 October 1869
18 Ocotber 1967

Schmalriede, Emil
30 November 1893
12 October 1915

Schmalriede, Adolph
November 1896
1896

Schmalriede, Rosa S
9 October 1858
31 July 1932

Schmalriede,Friedric
h
23 September 1857
27 January 1937

Mikeska, Jan
No dates given

Mikeska, Rosena
No date given

Mikeska, Rosa
1843
1929

Uhrik, John
1855
1912

Uhrik, Frances
1858
1916

Ripla, Franc
8 June 1833
1 March 1878

Arriens, Irma Louise
16 July 1924
No date given

Arriens, Otto M
28 May 1912
23 November 1979

Susen, Joe
1846
1894

Susen infant
Born & Died
1909

Susen, Edwin
23 July 1910
21 October 1918

Bravenec, Mathilda S
14 November 1912
No date given

Bravenec, John T
December 1906
3 September 1969

Susen, Theresa
23 April 1886
11 October 1967

Susen, Frank
12 February 1884
15 January 1952

Macuch, Anna
No date given
20 August 1968

Chernosky, John W
1861
1941

Chernosky, Mary F
1870
1942

Lubojasky, Lydia
2 January 1890
5 March 1955

Lubojasky, Will
8 June 1886
28 February 1956

Korenek infant
Born & Died
9 April 1942

Bravenec, Stephen
2 July 1877
21 March 1956

Bravenec, Frances
23 December 1877
27 February 1955

Shiller, Edward L
1898
1935

Shiller, Erline N
1927
1960

Shiller, Adina H
1909
1931

Shiller, Wincent
15 October 1850
20 April 1937

Shiller, Frances
15 December 1858
9 July 1930

Shiller, John J
6 October 1885
26 November 1910

Schiller, John S
15 July 1852
25 February 1935

Schiller,Frantiska
6 September 1857
6 May 1933

Siller, Frantisek
22 August 1896
3 April 1910

Janosky, Francis
4 October 1909
17 May 1969

Janosky, Rudolph
18 September 1906
4 January 1971

I-17

Mikeska, Julia A
17 August 1892
2 February 1981

Mikeska, Frank J
23 September 1893
27 November 1965

Tiemann, Annie
14 September 1887
7 November 1973

Tiemann, Willy
8 January 1883
24 July 1965

Janovsky, John T
25 January 1862
30 May 1943

Janovsky, Julia
4 January 1869
9 January 1945

Engelholm, Alvin E
30 March 1921
26 December 1921

Mikeska, Eugene J
31 August 1924
25 March 1932

Engleholm, Dennis
22 December 1925
13 June 1937

Arriens, Bertha
2 March 1886
31 December 1928

Arriens, Theodore
31 December 1879
11 November 1954

Pavelka, Alma
12 October 1886
5 February 1957

Pavelka, William
25 May 1883
14 August 1939

Janovsky, Amalia
17 January 1867
22 May 1957

Janovsky, Joe F
14 February 1864
23 January 1946

Miller, George W
11 May 1910
7 October 1981

Flick, Gladys Floy
27 July 1910
21 July 1969

Flick, Adolph
15 May 1908
17 April 1978

Mann, Freddie Wayne
7 April 1954
8 December 1968

Koppa, Ludve Frances
1 November 1892
16 May 1974

Bravenec, Jerry
8 December 1905
25 July 1977

Siller, Joseph B
21 February 1885
19 June 1913

Koppa, Vlastia Lydia
1 November 1896
No date given

Koppa, Thomas
2 February 1862
16 July 1935

Koppa, Annie
4 August 1860
21 November 1941

Schiller, John W
14 December 1888
22 July 1957

Schiller, Louise W
15 June 1889
15 November 1980

Scharli, Carl
24 March 1866
27 December 1898

Fila, Wilhemina
15 November 1872
22 April 1896

Korenek infant
Born & Died
9 April 1942

Mahlmann, Bailey B
16 January 1926
26 June 1977

Mahlmann, Norris R
15 May 1927
21 February 1980

Marcak, Karel
infant
No dates given

Marcak, Terezie
infant
No dates given

Bacica, John
1867
1942

I-18

SVAJDA-HEJL CEMETERY

Location of Svajda cemetery: Starting from the town of Nelsonville, go out FM 141 one mile and turn left on the first gravel road, go 100 yards to a gate on the left.

Hejl, Josef
16 January 1813
22 September 1892

Hejl, Lydia
10 May 1820
19 June 1896

THOMPSON CEMETERY

Location of Thompson cemetery: Starting from the town of Bellville, go north on Hwy 36 take FM 159 west to Oak Hill. Turn right and cemetery is to the left.

Dolesal, A.B.
14 February 1872
3 November 1904

Garrett, Elizabeth L
No dates given

Faucelle, C.H.
9 March 1830
20 June 1878

Logan, Tobitha
29 January 1848
3 February 1881

Logan, Aaron M
1 January 1800
13 September 1881

Wennweser, Sallie
6 March 1863
19 January 1887

Willis, Viola Isabell
29 November 1876
29 January 1877

Logan, Mattie P
20 March 1881
3 October 1882

Infant unknown
22 August 1884
24 August 1884

Logan, John W
26 February 1875
25 March 1885

Thompson unknown
No dates given

Thompson, James H
No date given
1887

Thompson, Ida Jane
9 December 1875
25 February 1878

Daughtrey,Isabella
1831
17 December 1886

Daughtrey, James
18 July 1823
20 December 1899

Daughtrey,Anna Kamas
1850
29 June 1905

Olsen, Dorothea
15 August 1829
28 February 1906

Daughtrey,Isabella
1831
17 December 1886

Thompson infant
20 June 1892
25 June 1892

Minton, S.A.
15 December 1841
13 May 1899

Hinze, Jesse
2 June 1900
12 November 1900

3 unmarked graves

I-19

UECKERT FAMILY CEMETERY #1

Location of Ueckert family cemetery: Go west from Bellville on Hwy. 159 approximately 5 miles to the V. R. Ueckert farm. The Cemetery is about 300 yards north of Hwy. 159.

Ueckert, Mrs. L.W.A. 5 January 1810 7 March 1906	Ueckert, Emma Hohle 14 December 1865 14 March 1901	Ueckert, Fritz 27 December 1890 3 January 1891
	Ueckert, Mathilde 10 September 1892 23 August 1898	Ueckert, Ferdinand 5 February 1895 16 February 1895

ZETTEL CEMETERY

Location of Zettel cemetery: Go west of Nelsonville on Hwy 159 approximately 1.5 miles to FM 2754. Take a right turn back at a sharp angle and go approximately 2\10 miles to Cemetery road. Turn left and you will find Zettel cemetery on the left side of the road, across from the National Cemetery which is on the right.

Walcik, Edward 23 June 1896 5 June 1962	Zettel, William 24 February 1887 19 June 1972	Zettel, Marie 25 January 1885 15 February 1885
Walcik, Emilie A 26 December 1904 30 October 1978	Zettel, Louise 22 February 1887 11 November 1967	Zettel, Francis 27 July 1883 2 July 1972
Zettel, Emma Anna 1909 1983	lin B 5 November 1919 22 February 1948	Zettel, Fritz H 9 December 1879 17 October 1956
 1 November 1903 5 April 1979	Zettel, Albina 31 July 1933 11 October 1935	Zettel, Gustav 2 January 1881 12 March 1955
Zettel, Tillie 18 January 1904 13 September 1970	Zettel, Charles J 18 July 1892 21 September 1973	Zettel, Therese 22 July 1884 24 May 1963
Zettel, Johnnie B 12 November 1924 21 June 1974	Zettel, Albina 31 March 1908 6 August 1963	Zettel, Anna 2 December 1859 15 October 1942
Zettel, Willie J 4 September 1908 15 November 1979	Zettel infant 20 August 1916 22 August 1916	Zettel, Fritz 6 August 1855 22 February 1907
Zettel, Annie A 23 March 1925 8 March 1973	Zettel infant Born & Died 20 August 1916	Zettel, Frank J 25 November 1889 6 March 1968
Slacik, Charles 22 June 1877 4 April 1955	Slacik, Anna 20 July 1882 6 January 1960	Zettel, Oscar 28 December 1905 8 May 1906
		6 Unmarked grave

I-20

After the book “Cemeteries of Austin County, Texas” was printed, O. B. Shelburne completed extensive research and restoration of three Shelburne family cemeteries in the Mill Creek forks area. A summary of the headstones and inferred burials as compiled by O. B. Shelburne follows:

John Shelburne Cemetery located west of Bleiberville at the original Shelburne homestead:

1. Jane Dunkin Sept. 20, 1771 to August 19, 1851
2. Mary Elizabeth Shelburne March 29, 1830 to June 9, 1845
3. Nancy L. Shelburne September 20, 1797 to June 3, 1858
4. John Pamplin Shelburne December 20, 1790 to November 20, 1791 (?)
5. unmarked grave, probably James Henry Shelburne August 9, 1826 to >1880.
6. John S. Minton April 3, 1852 to February 1, 1876
7. eroded headstone reported to read John Minton
8. Jane K. Shelburne Minton Jan. 12, 1816 to April 6, 1874
9. Alfred Minton 1809 to October 26, 1852
10. apparent headstone fragments possibly Henrietta America Minton 1868 to 1869

Samuel Shelburne Cemetery located about 2 miles north of Industry:

1. Leila A. Shelburne Jan. 14, 1871 to Sept. 14, 1873
2. John W. Dixon Dec. 16, 1870 to Feb. 2, 187 ? (2 or 3)
3. William Bell Shelburne Apr. 3, 1854 to Mar. 21, 1863
4. Ernest K. Shelburne Aug. 26, 1862 to Apr. 25, 1864
5. Georgia Anna Shelburne April 21, 1868 to Aug. 17, 1876
6. Samuel Allen Dixon July 22, 1876 to July 9, 1877
7. unmarked possible headstone of Ida Shelburne ca. 1865 to 1865-69
8. Nancy L. Shelburne Feb. 4, 1853 to Oct. 26, 1880
9. infant daughter of G.B. and Juliet A. Dixon Jan. 7 to Mar 7, 1878

William Shelburne Cemetery located off Zettle Road near Nelsonville ; same “Shelburne Cemetery” in book “Cemeteries of Austin County, Texas”

1. area of field stones possibly graves of children Mary Calpernia and William F. Shelburne
2. William L. Shelburne Jan. 24, 1857 to Feb. 2, 1878
3. unmarked well defined fieldstone outline, perhaps William’s daughter Kate 1872 to ca. 1881.
4. Mattie James Sept. 4, 1882 to Sept. 13, 1882
5. Mary Catherine Shelburne July 2, 1832 to July 23, 1893
6. unmarked but well defined fieldstone probably John Pamplin Shelburne 1856 to March 1896.

Czech Family Origins

	Surnames in Cemeteries in the Forks of Mill Creek showing places of family origin				
Ref: records of Rev. Jindrich Juren as reported in "Czech Footprints across the bluebonnet fields of Texas" by Albert J. Blaha, 1983					
Andreas		Keener		Smilek	
Arriens		Koppa	Vycovice, Zadverice	Stalbaum	Zadverice
Bacica	Rokatnice (Vsetin)	Korenek	Hovezi		
Baletka	Hostalkova (Vsetin)	Krause		Stasny	Ratibor near Vsetin
Banks		Krizan		Stepan	Hostalkova near Vsetin
Barnett		Kroulik	Voderady	Surovik	
Bartay		Kudlacek	Divnic, Zadverice	Susen	Liptal, Ratibor, Vsetin
Beathe		Lancer		Syptak	(Siptak) Zadverice
Beckmann		Leps		Taska	
Bell		Lesikar	Cermna	Thompson	
Bernhausen		Lewis		Tiemann	
Bethany		Lindeman		Tison	
Blackwell		Liska		Tylajdka	
Blum		Logan		Ueckert	
Bouldin		Lubojasky	Chicbun	Uherka	
Bravenec	Katerinice (Vsetin)	Macat	Cermna	Uhrik	Zadverice
Broughton		Mahlmann		Vacusek	
Burns		Malechek		Walcik	
Cernocka		Mann		Walicek	
Chaka		Manzel		Wennweser	
Chaloupka	Cermna, Nepomucky	Manzelka		Wernli	
Chernosky	Vsetin	Marcak		Williamson	
Coufal		Maresh	Cermna	Willis	
Daughtrey		Masar		Wunderling	
Davis		McKinney		Zettle	
Dean		Mehner			
Dekalb		Meinke			
Dixon		Mikeska	Zadverice, Luskova, Jasene	Balousek	Zadverice
Dolesal		Milberger		Langer	Cermna
Drevojanek		Miller		Motl	Cermna
Duebbe		Minton		Jezek	Cermna
Dunkin		Muery		Haisler	Cermna
Edgar		Ogg			
Elsik	Hostalkova, Zadverice	Olsen			
Engelholm		Pavelek	Rajnochovice Mor. dist. Holeshev		
Esterak	Vsetin				
Faucelle		Peters	Bordovice		
Fick		Plasek			
Fila		Pochmann			
Flake		Pomykal	Zadverice		
Flick		Reed			
Fraktiser		Renner			
Garrett		Richard			
Gerhart		Ripple	Cermna		
Glaser		Roesler			
Glinger		Rychlik			
Golan		Sailer			
Grebe		Scharli			
Haedge		Schiller	Cermna		
Hanka		Schimara			
Hartman		Schmalreide			
Harvel		Schmara			
Hasting		Schmidt			
Hejl	Cermna	Schovasja			
Hinze		Schramm			
Hochbaum		Schroeder			
Holba	Zadverice	Schupak	(Supak) Horzenkov		
Huff		Sebesta	Lipyne, Zadverice		
James		Seda			
Janecek	Dzbanov	Sefcik	Lipyne, Zadverice		
Janek	Hodslavice	Shelburne			
Janosky	Mistek	Shupak			
Jochec		Sisa	Zadverice		
Jurik	Zadverice	Slacik			
Kaase		Sloupensky			
Kamas	Katerinice	Slovak	Vysovice near Vsetin		

Map of northeastern Bohemia, Litomysl and Lanskroun Districts, Czech Republic, showing villages of origin of Texas immigrants.

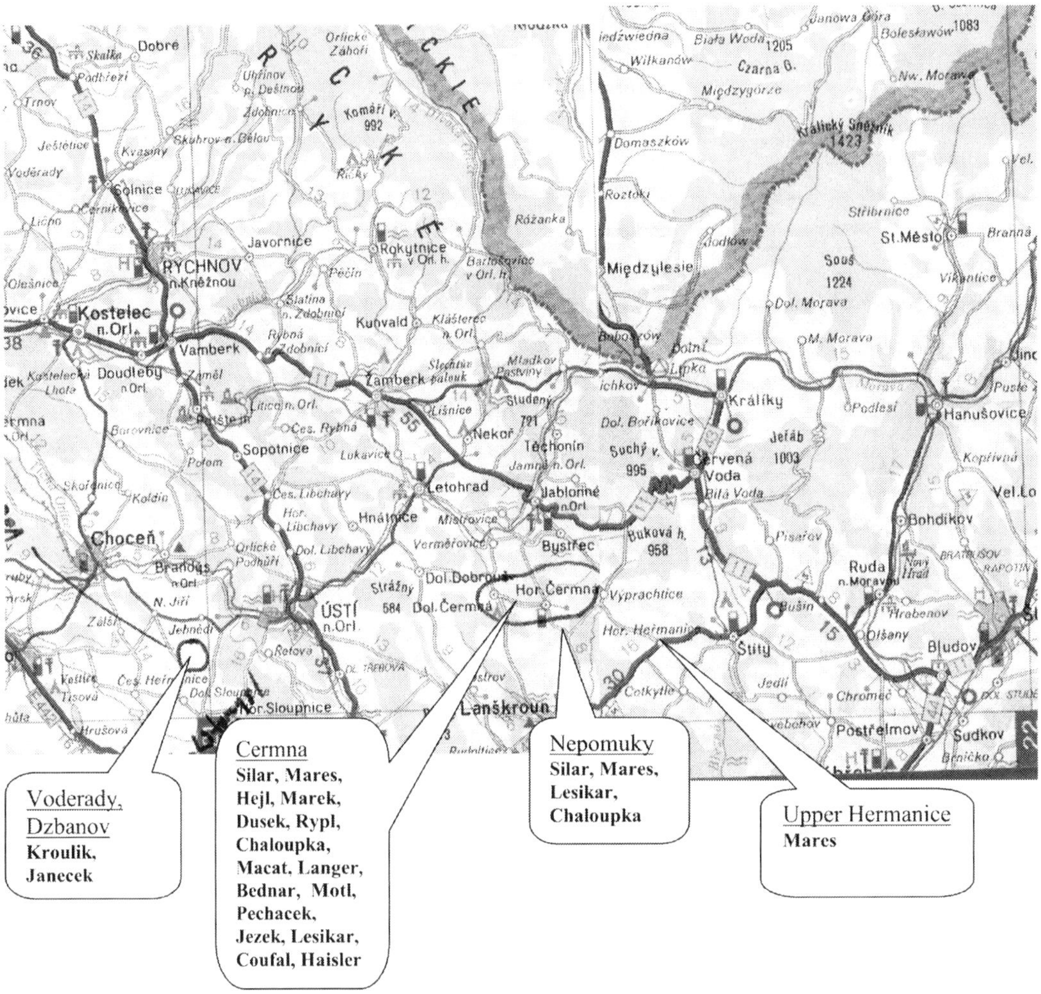

Map of eastern Moravia (Czech Republic) showing origins of Texas immigrants

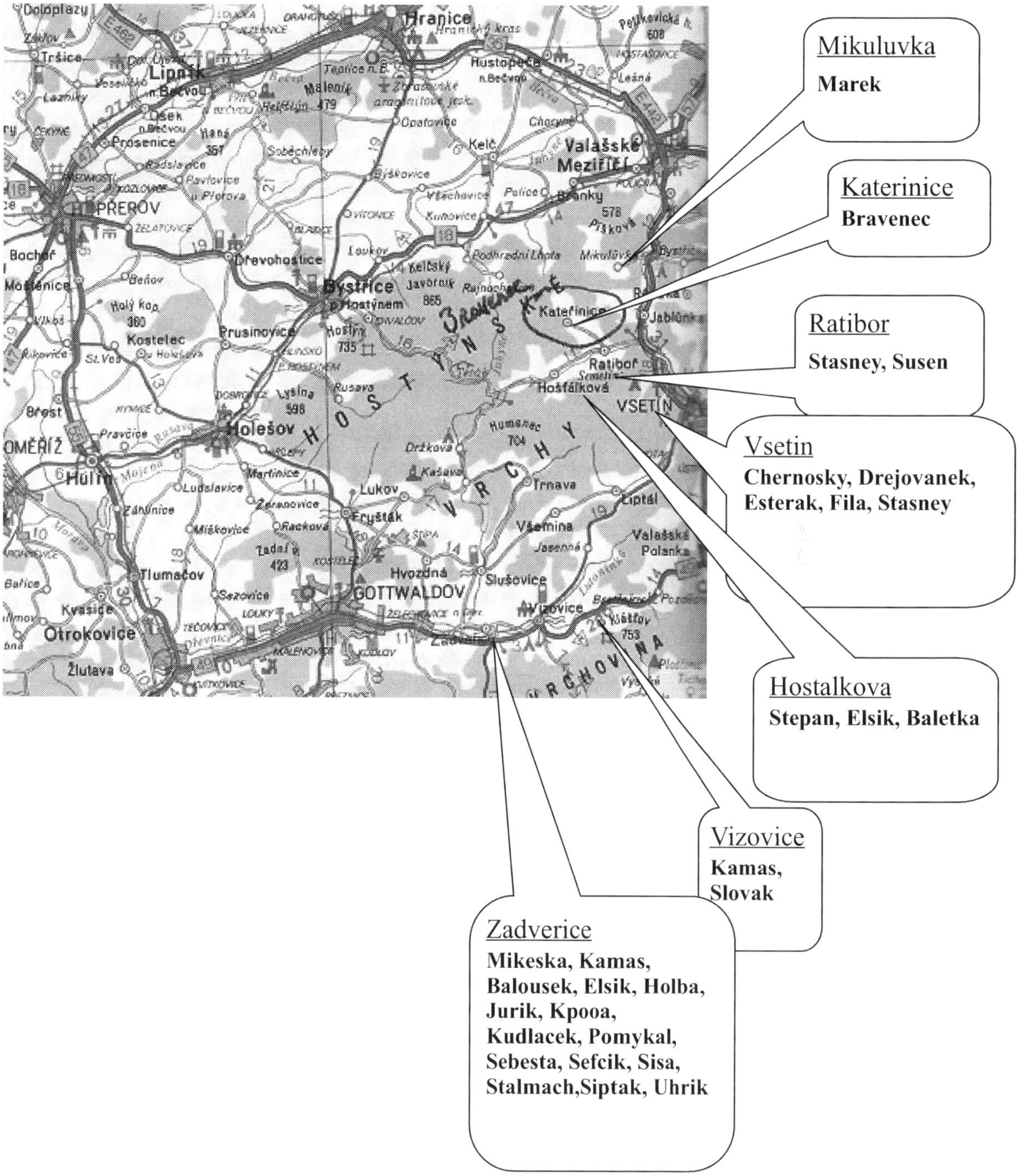

Photos from Voderady and Dzbanov, Litomysl District, Czech Republic, July 2004

Protestant Church in Sloupnice (attended from Voderady and Dzbanov)

Looking down on Katerinice from House #115,

home to five generations of Bravenec family

Austin County Land Grants

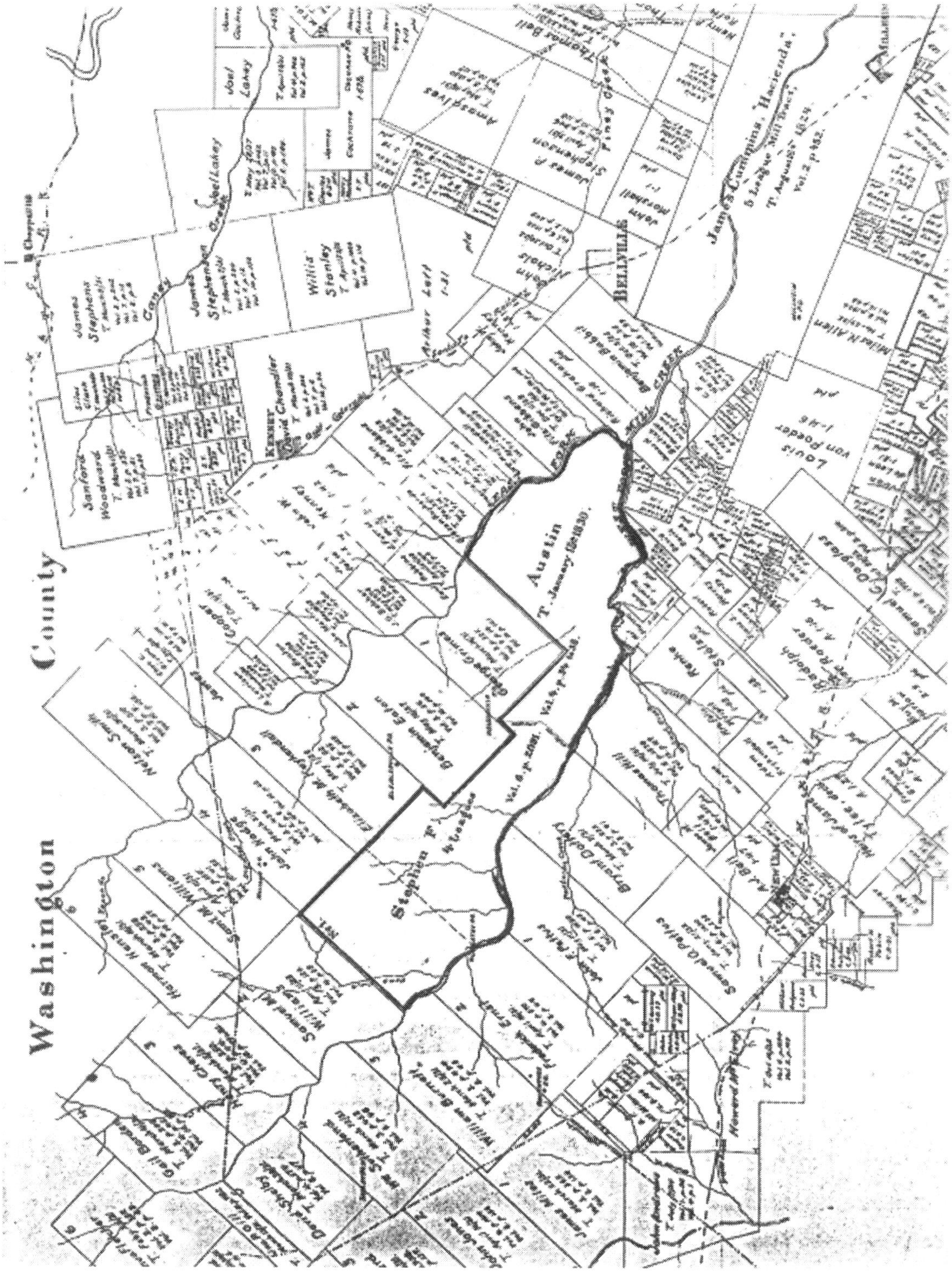

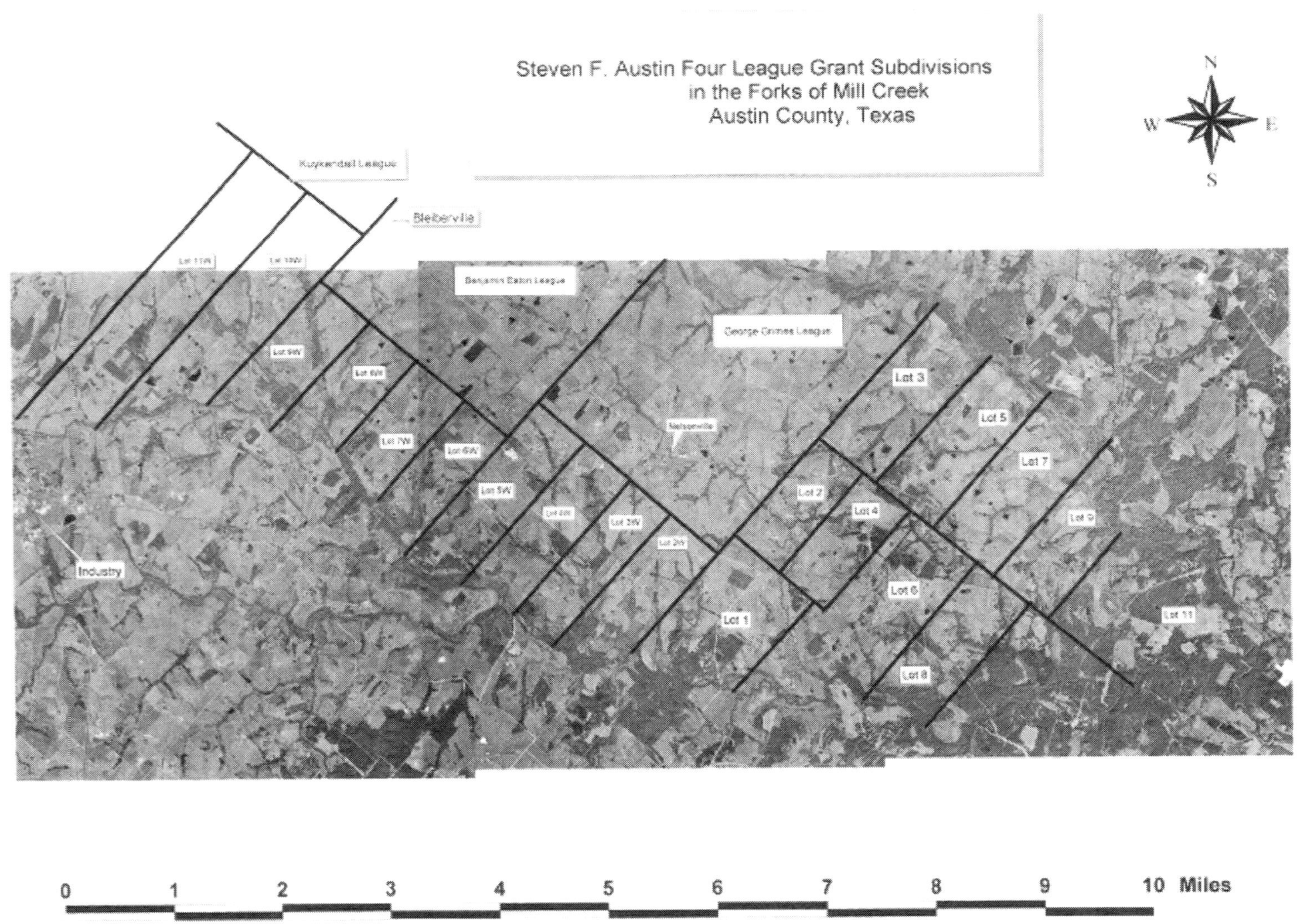
Steven F. Austin Four League Grant Subdivisions
in the Forks of Mill Creek
Austin County, Texas
N
W
E
S
Kuykendall League
Bleiberville
Benjamin Eaton League
George Grimes League
Nelsonville
Industry
Lot 9W
Lot 8W
Lot 7W
Lot 6W
Lot 5W
Lot 3W
Lot 2W
Lot 1
Lot 2
Lot 3
Lot 4
Lot 5
Lot 6
Lot 7
Lot 8
Lot 9
Lot 11
0
1
2
3
4
5
6
7
8
9
10 Miles

Guy Bryan Plat of S. F. Austin Four League Grant

Showing towns and early land purchases / settlers

Plat from Austin County Deed Records Book IJ page 156

Filed April 17th 1855 at 3 P. M. Recorded May 7, 1855 at 3 P. M.

Jas C Francis Clk A C Ct.

- - - - - - - - - - -

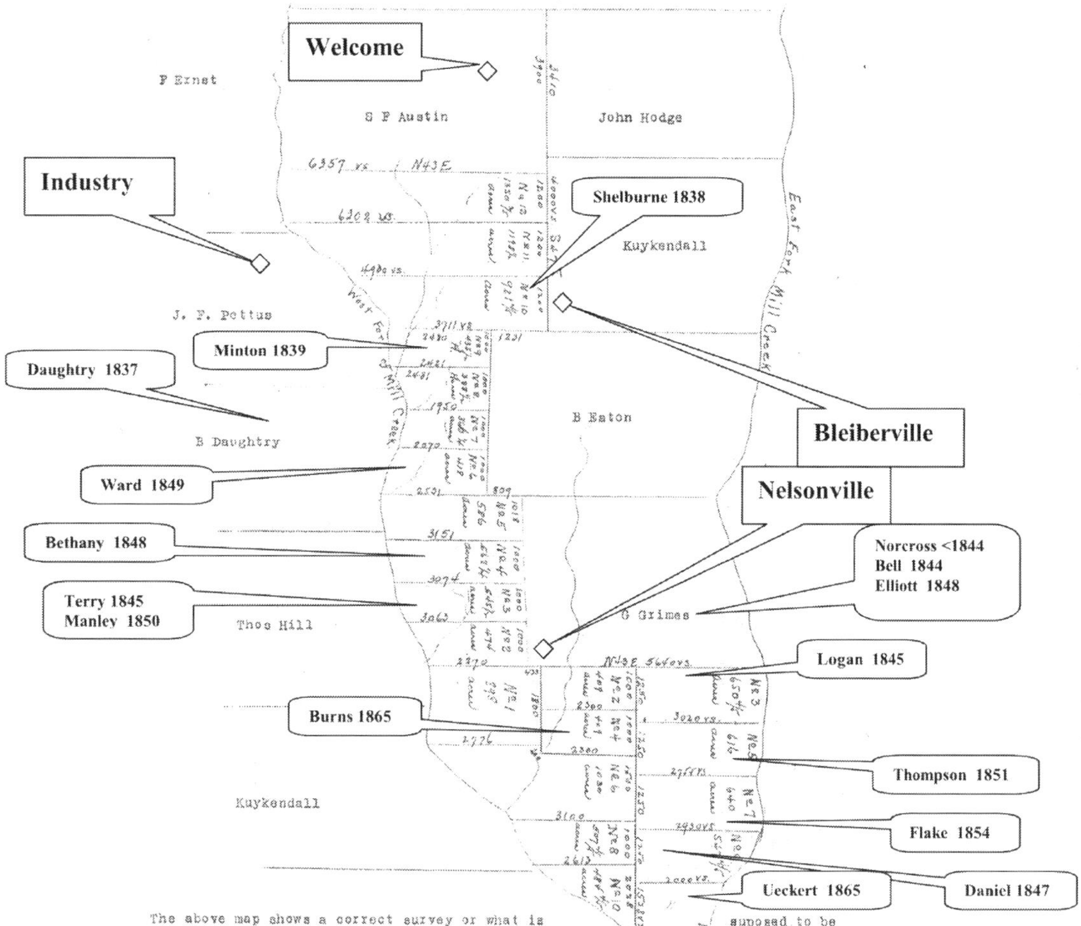

The above map shows a correct survey or what is supposed to be a correct survey of lands in the fork of Mill Creek in Austin County conveyed to me in Trust by James F Perry Emily M Perry Wm C Hill and Eliza M Hill by deed dated 15 September A. D. 1846. I have made sales to different persons in refference to the above survey and I now record the map so that deeds made in reference to it may be understood by all parties interested

Witness my hand & scrawl for seal this 17th day of April 1855

Guy M Bryan

Filed April 17th 1855 at 10 A M Recorded May 8th 1855 at 4 P M.

Jas C Francis Clk A C

Money Order from Nelsonville Post Office July 6, 1897

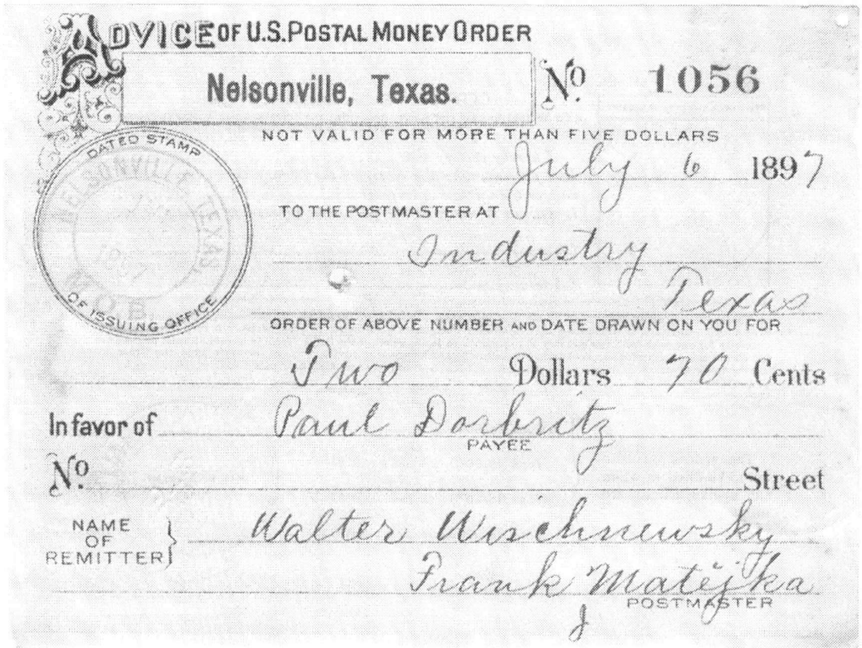

ADVICE OF U.S. POSTAL MONEY ORDER

Nelsonville, Texas. No. 1056

NOT VALID FOR MORE THAN FIVE DOLLARS

July 6 1897

TO THE POSTMASTER AT Industry Texas

ORDER OF ABOVE NUMBER AND DATE DRAWN ON YOU FOR

Two Dollars 70 Cents

In favor of Paul Dorbritz PAYEE

No. Street

NAME OF REMITTER Walter Wischnewsky

Frank Matějka POSTMASTER

DATED STAMP OF ISSUING OFFICE

NELSONVILLE TEXAS 1897 M.O.B.

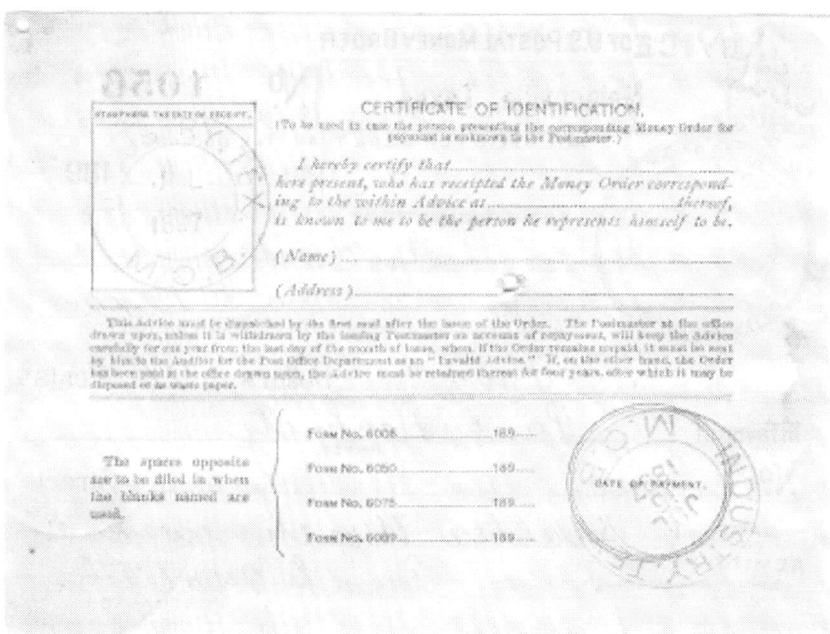

STAMP HERE THE DATE OF RECEIPT.

CERTIFICATE OF IDENTIFICATION.

(To be used in case the person presenting the corresponding Money Order for payment is unknown to the Postmaster.)

I hereby certify that ....
here present, who has receipted the Money Order corresponding to the within Advice at .... *thereof, is known to me to be the person he represents himself to be.*

(Name) ....

(Address) ....

This Advice must be dispatched by the first mail after the issue of the Order. The Postmaster at the office drawn upon, unless it is withdrawn by the issuing Postmaster on account of repayment, will keep the Advice carefully for one year from the last day of the month of issue, when, if the Order remains unpaid, it must be sent by him to the Auditor for the Post Office Department as an "Invalid Advice." If, on the other hand, the Order has been paid at the office drawn upon, the Advice must be retained thereat for four years, after which it may be disposed of as waste paper.

The spaces opposite are to be filled in when the blanks named are used.

Form No. 6008..............189....
Form No. 6050..............189....
Form No. 6075..............189....
Form No. 6089..............189....

DATE OF PAYMENT.

"Nelsonville Street-Car" Postcard
"Joe Jezek General Merchandise"

Ca. 1910

Driver: Joe Jezek
Back Row Standing: Ben Pavelka or Edwin Bravenec
Middle Row : Frank Jezek, Charles Chernosky, Willie Pavelka, John Balusek
Front Row: John J. Bravenec, Ignac Chernosky, Joe Balusek, Dr. John Kroulik

Nelsonville Main Street, early 1900's
Dr. John Kroulik Office, mercantile store

Nelsonville C. S. P. S. Hall - 1890

First Floor - Dance Hall
Second Floor - School Room

Nelsonville S. P. J. S. T. Hall

John Pamplin Shelburne homestead – built 1838, photo ca. 1875

First dwelling built on the Steven F. Austin Four League Grant
Originally typical frontier double log cabin with open "dog trot" area between two rooms. Log walls still visible under porch. Vertical lines faintly visible in this photograph indicate where dog trot opening was later enclosed.

Shelburne Descendents - 1895

Top L-R: Sarah Alexander Glenn, Robert Minton, Georgia Shelburne, Annie Bell, Nona Shelburne, Olla Bethany, Emma Bethany, Bessie Bell, Calpernia Shelburne, James Robert Thompson.
Middle L-R: Mollie Perkins Shelburne, Calpernia Bell Bethany, Sarah Adeline Bell Bethany, Sarah Pamplin Shelburne Glenn in chair, Virginia Ann Minton Thompson, Rolfe V. Bethany behind Wells Mathew Bethany in white shirt, Annie L. Dement Bethany holding son Gus John English Bethany.
Seated L-R: Henry Fordtran Glenn, Ethyl Cumings, Ethyl Bethany, Nena McDade, Bessie Brookfield Fordtran, Artie Bethany.

1913 Maifest at Nelsonville SPJST Hall

King Henry Ripple, Queen Tillie Chernosky
Front, L-R: Elmo Chernosky, Lexie Minton, Joe and Frances Blazek
Back, L-R: Edwin Stalmach, Joe Sula, Annie Kamas, Leona Stalmach, Edwin Bravenec, Vlasta Koppa, Charles Motl, Hilda Balusek, Vera Svajda, Willie Kamas

Nelsonville Orcherstra - 1914

Photo taken in home of Dr. John Kroulik

Adolph Dahse (Standing with base fiddle)
Frank Bednar (back to camera)
Joe J. Sula (back to dresser)
Edward Bartay (in corner)
Dr. John Kroulik (with violin)

Pictures on the wall are Kroulik family members of the area. From left to right are Karel and Rosalie Silar Lesikar of New Bremen, Jan and Frantiska Pachr Kroulik of Schoenau, and Thresa Kroulik Lewis. The small picture on the dresser on the extreme left is of Mrs. Jan (Rosalie Coufal) Silar.

Saturday Afternoon Card Game

Right to Left: Frank Supak, (unknown), John Moudry, Willie Krause, Ben Motl, Frank Blazek

Nelsonville Young People

1913 picnic

Back Row: Rose Shiller, Edwin Janecek, Joe Sula, Leona Stalmach, Charles Shiller, Helen Huber, Charles Stalmach, Emilie Shiller, Hermina Uhrik, Henry Ripple

Middle Row: on left, Ed. Uhrik

"Beer Drinkers"

Saturday Afternoon in Nelsonville

Boys Swimming in Ash Hole, Mill Creek

Back 3: Sayler, Willie Kamas and Haedge
Middle Long Row: Ben Motl, Ed Blazek, Tom Kamas, Ed Stalmach, Otto Krause, John Kamas
In Front: Charles Motl

First Automobile to Appear in Nelsonville
Stalmach's Yard on a Sunday in 1913
Paige Auto Owned by J. F. Baier of Brenham
Front (L-R): Joe Baier, Earline Baier, Louise Lesikar Baier
Back (L-R): Henry Ripple, Esther Lesikar, Gardenia Lesikar, Olga Kroulik Quitta, Leona Stalmach

Cotton Chopping Time in Nelsonville

Nelsonville SPJST Members - 1915

(Identification on next four pages)

I. OBRAZ ODBOČKY Č. N. S. V NELSONVILLE.

První řada. Wm. Kamas, Fr. Plášek, Jan Čermák, J. S. Schiller, Jan Bravenec, Jos. Holba, Jos. Ježek, Jos. Kamas, Karel Stupka, Fr. Šiša, Jos. Coufal, W. S. Schiller, Jan G. Mikeska, Hugo Fischer, F.B. Mareš, Jos. Schiller, Vinc. Bednář a Fr. Máčat. Ve druhé řadě. Štěp. Bravenec, Jan F. Mikeska, Jan V. Schiller, Karel Šebesta, Tom Surovik, Jos. Mareš, Fr. Lala, Jan Bačica, Fr. Šušen, E. Uhřík, J.C. Minton, Vinc. Kašpárek, Ed. Bravenec, Karel A. Schiller, Jan Juřík a Jan Esteřák. Ve třetí řadě. J.J. Bravenec, Emil Leškar, Wm. Mareš, F.A. Mikeska, Jos. Slačík, Jan Zajíček, Jan Surovik, Fr. Šebesta, Jos. F. Janovský, Jos. Šebesta, Fr. Šupák, Jan Šušen, Wm. Pavelka, Dr. Jan Kroulík a Jan Stalmach. Ve čtvrté řadě. Karel Pomykal, Fr. Pavelka, Tom Bravenec, Fr. J. Mikeska, Jan Bravenec ml., Fr. Bednář, Tom M. Kamas, F. Schiller, Otto Krause, Tom Kopa, Mart. Kutěj. Dole v páté řadě jsou hoši: John Kroulík, Alfred Kroulík, Jan Bravenec a Jan J. Šebesta.

II. OBRAZ ODBOČKY Č. N. S. V NELSONVILLE.

Sl. Emilie Schillerova, sl. Tillie Bravencova, sl. Lydie Stalmachova, sl. Ella Schillerova, sl. Lexie Mintonova, sl. Lilie Schillerova, sl. Sadie Marešova, sl. Anna Lalova, pí. J. Krausová, pí. J. Mintonová, sl. Vinc. Esteřákova, pí. J. Kroulíková, pí K. Pomykalová, sl. Anna Kamasova, sl. Anna Marešova, sl. Teresie Plaškova, sl. Marie Bravencova, sl. Marie Surovikova. Ve druhé řadě, pí. F. Plašková, pí. F. Šebestová, pí. K. Šebestová, pí. Tom Bravencová, pí. J. Čermáková, pí. Jan Juříková, pí F. Supáková, pí. J. Bravencová, pí. J. Zajíčková, pí Fr. Mikesková, pí. Wm. Marešová, pí. J. Stalmachová, pí. Jos. Kamasová, pí. J.S. Schillerová, sl. Rosalie Suroviková, sl. Frant. Surovikova. Ve třetí řadě. pí. J.J. Bravencová, pí. Tom Suroviková, pí. Fr. Lalová, pí. Jos. Šebestová, pí. Louise Lišková, pí. Jos. Slačíková, pí. Jan V. Schilerová, pí J. Ježková, pí J. Suroviková, pí. W.S. Schillerová, pí. St. Bravencová, pí. Ed. Bravencová, pí. Karel Schillerová, pí. Jan J. Bravencová, pí. J. Janovská, pí. J. Merešová. Ve čtvrté řadě. Vlasta Šebestova, Anna Liškova, Gracie Ježkova, Olga Surovikova, Rosie Surovikova, Jan Surovik, Emil Surovik, Olga Šebestova, Stanislava Surovikova.

Odbočka Č.N.S. v Nelsonville, Texas.

Nelsonville je malé městečko vzdálené 9 mil od Bellville, okresního sídla okresu Austin. Naleză se tu jeden obchod, ev. kostel a 2 síně spolkové, celé okolí pak je osazeno našimi krajany a Němci. Hned na počátku činnosti Nár. Sdružení se někteří krajané zdejší přihlásili k Odb. v Bleiberville, avšak ku zorganisování samostatné Odb. nedošlo až v roce 1918. Po schůzi řádu SPJST dne 11. srpna členové Fr. Bednář a Fr. Šebesta promluvili ku četně shromážděným sestrám a bratřím a povzbudili 20 posluchačů k založení Odbočky. Prvními úředníky byli zvoleni: Fr. Šebesta za předsedu, J. W. Ježek pokladníkem a slč. A. M. Lálová tajemnicí. Uzavřeno pak svolati další schůzi na den 25 srpna. Ta byla dobře navštívena a přihlásilo se dalších 48 členů. Tu pak byli zvoleni trvalí úředníci a sice: Fr. Bednář předsedou, dr. J. J. Kroulík pokladníkem, slč. A. M. Lálová tajemnicí a Fr. Šebesta důvěrníkem.

Ve schůzi odbývané 8. září se přihlásilo dalších 75 členů a mimo schůze bylo získáno 12 členů, tak že počet všech dostoupil 164. Přednášku tu měl jednou pan J. M. Vondráček z Caldwell, která byla s velkým zájmem vyslechnuta.

Velmi živý zájem objevili členové při sbírání bavlny pro Státní Bazar v Taylor. Krajané Jos. Šefčík, Vil. Kamas a Jan Bravenec ml. se uvolili sbírati bavlnu a nikde nebyli odmítnuti, tak že ji sebrali 2848 liber, z níž udělány dva žoky, z nichž jeden vážil 537, druhý 480 liber. Jeden z těch balíků zdarma vyčistil p. Otto Wienke při New Ulm, druhý p. Hugo Fischer v Bellville. Mimo to přispěli krajanky a krajané z okolí Nelsonvillu na Stát. Bazar různými dárky v ceně $14 a $19.50 na hotovosti. Také Národní daň v okolí vybírána, která vynesla $93.75.

Zvláštní schůze svolána byla na den 8. září, při níž byli členové Odb. fotografováni pro Památník. Byl též pozván k tomu pan Vondráček z Caldwell, který četnému shromáždění důtklivou řečí vysvětlil účel, jaký sleduje Čes. Nár. Sdružení. Ještě při této příležitosti se přihlásilo dalších 75 členů, tak že v širém tom okolí zůstalo málo našinců, kteří by na sklonku roku 1918 nebyli členy Odbočky Č. N. S.

Mimo to však byla po řeči p. Vondráčka založena od přítomných žen organisace Včelek, která brzy získala 37 členkyň. Tyto sebraly v krátké době $85.55 ve prospěch našich vojínů na Sibiři, jimž mimo to vyplnily 6 kabelek různými potřebami. Též sbírka na tabák vojínům československé armády vynesla $12.90. Na Červ. Kříž, jakož i pro ostatní dobročinné společnosti bylo mezi členy Odb. hojných příspěvků sebráno, jen že se o tom podrobné záznamy nezachovaly. Jen členské příspěvky obnášely $207.25. Členy Odbočky byli:

Jos. Cuřal, J. W. Ježek a choť, Jan Schiller ml. a choť, Frank Bednář a choť, Jos. Liška, Alois Joch[illegible] se Jochec, Gilbert Jochec, Jan Mikeska a choť, [illegible] reš a choť a dcera, W. S. Schiller, choť, syn a 3 d[illegible] B. Mareš, choť a dcera, Frank Lala st., choť a dc[illegible]

Mikeska, choť a 2 synové, Jan Surovík st., choť, 3 dcery a 2 synové, Jan Stalmach, choť, syn a dcera, Will. Kamas, Wm. Mareš a choť, J. L. Minton, choť a syn. Dále: Karel Šebesta a choť, Jos. Kamas, choť, syn a dcera, Frank Šebesta a choť, Jan Estelák a 3 dcery, Frank Šupák a choť, st. Františka Šebesta, Rev. Anton Motyčka, Martin Kutej, Jos. Slačík a choť, Jan Zapěck a choť, Dr. Jan Kroulík, choť a 2 synové, Jan Bravenec st., choť a syn, Jos. F. Janovský a choť, Vinc. Kašpárek, Tom. Surovík, choť, 4 dcery a syn, Tomáš Bravenec, choť a dcera, Jan Šefčík, Tom. Koppa, Herm. Krause a choť, Chas. Stupka a choť, Ed Uhřík, Emil Leškar, Frank A. Mikeska a choť, Hugo Fisher a choť, Jan Schiller st. a choť, Jan L. Jurík a choť, Otto Krause, Jos. Shiller, choť a syn, Ed. Bravenec a choť, Frank Mačat a choť, Jos. Šebesta, choť, syn a 2 dcery, pí. Aloisie Lišková, dcera a syn, Jos. Holba, Jan Čermák a choť, pí. Al. Krause, Frank Plašek, choť a dcera, Wm. Pavelka, Chas. A. Shiller a choť, Lydie Janovská, J. J. Bravenec, choť, syn a dcera, Frank Mareš, Chas. Pomikal a choť, Jan Susen, Frank Pavelka, Frank Susen, Ed. G. Bartay, Štěpán Bravenec a choť, Jan Sinel, Tom. Kozlovský a choť, Adolf Walíček a choť, sl. Gracie Ježkova, Vinc. Bednář, Frank Šiša a choť, Jan Bačica, Will. Krause, choť a syn, Frank Blažek a choť, Jos. Šefčík a choť. —

Bleiberville S.P.J.S.T. Lodge #33 - 1914

Bleiberville S.P.J.S.T. Lodge #33 - 1914
Top: Charlie Slacik, Vencil Broz, John Jurchak, John Slacik, Joe Siptak, William Stepan, Joe Stepan from Kenney, ?, Joe Balteke, Suadja, Suadja,
Willie Susen, Willie Schimera, Joe Koppa
Middle: Joe Schimera, ?, Joe Slovak, ?, John Jurchak Sr., Tom Mikeska, Frank Schovajsa, ?, Joe Liska, Paul Surough, Mrs. Paul Surough, Mrs. Joe Slovak
Bottom: Vlasta Stepan, Mrs. Joe (Minnie Stepan) Schovajsa, Mrs. John (Rosa Stepan) Gebhardt, Mrs. Charlie Siptak, Mrs. Frances Mikeska,
Mrs. John Baletka, Charlie Siptak, Nadsu, John Schovajsa, Mrs. John Schovajsa, Mrs. Tom Mikeska, Mrs. Willie Stepan, Anne Siptak, Mrs. Gebhardt

Nelsonville Unity of the Brethren Church
First Sunday School Class - 1912

Top: Tom Kamas, Edwin Stalmach, Willie Kamas, Joe Motycka, Sam Kutej, Birdie Shiller, John Kamas, Edmund Stalmach
3rd: Seyman, Hilda Balusek, Leona Stalmach, Lydia Stalmach, Annie Kamas, Winnie Esterak, Mary Kamas, Rosie Kutej, Rosalie Esterak, Rosie Balusek
2nd: Lexie Minton, Lilian Chernosky, Julia Supak, Carrie Balusek, Theresa Shiller, Vlasta Maresh, Lydia Maresh, Theresa Blasek, O. Surovik
First: Otto Chernosky, Alvin Maresh, Edwin Maresh, Eddie Shiller

Confirmation at Nelsonville Church
Rev. Anton Motycka

Confirmation Classes at Nelsonville Brethren Church

Above: John Anton Stepan (seated 3rd from right)
Ruth Maresh (left of Rev. Motchka)
Otto Stepan (seated 2nd from left)

Below: Lillie Maresh (seated 1st from right)
Milady Maresh (seated 4th from right)

Confirmation at Nelsonville Brethren Church - 1914

Rev. Anton Motycka

Back Row 3rd and 7th from left: Albina Surovik (Krupala) and Annie Surovik (Bennett)

Confirmation at Nelsonville Brethren Church - 8/19/1923

Rev. Anton Motycka

Top row from right 2nd Miroslav Petreusek, 4th Jerry Sebesta, 6th Henry Sebesta
Middle row from right 3rd Adolf Krizen, 5th Rose Surovic

Nelsonville School - 1907 - 1908

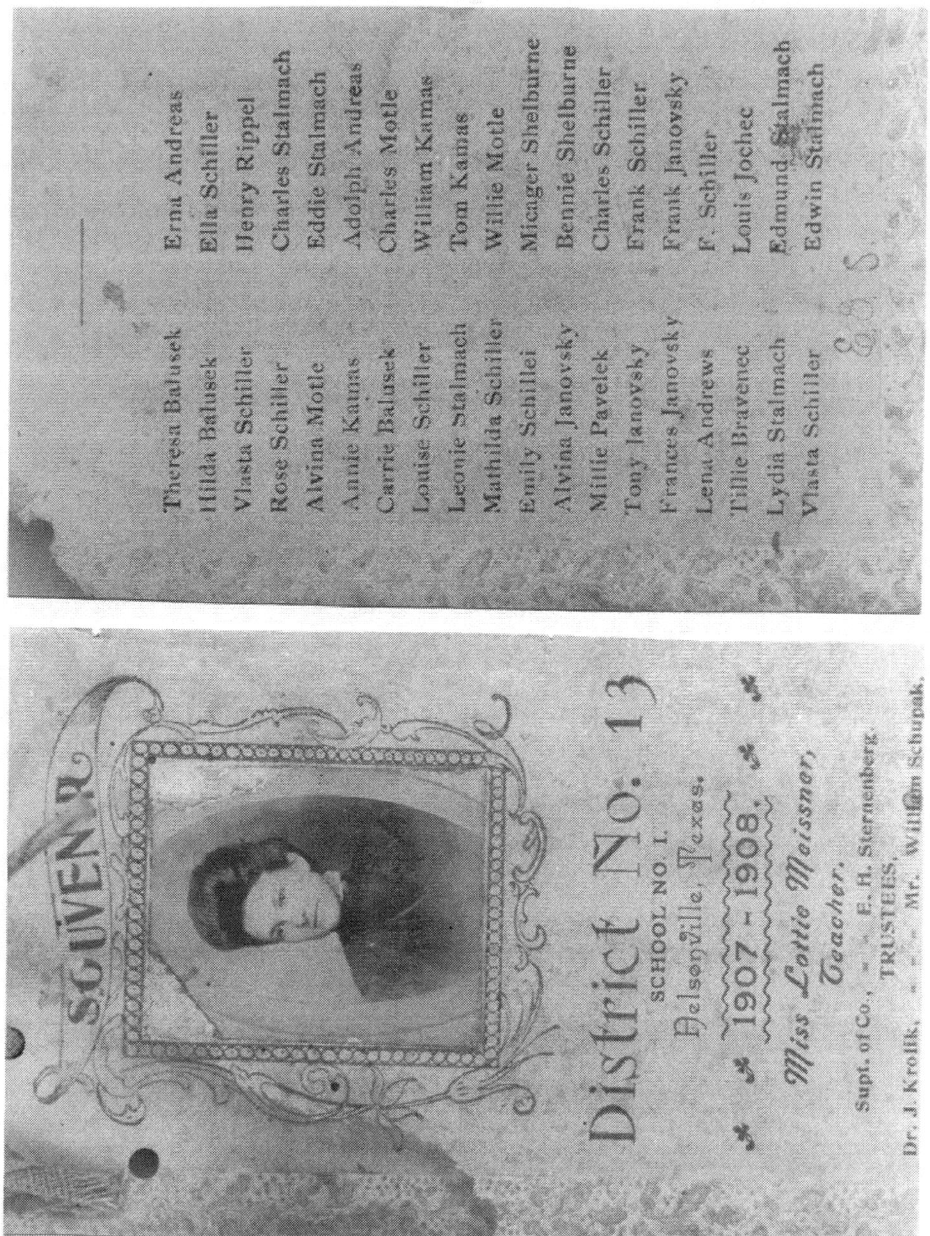

SOUVENIR

District No. 13

SCHOOL NO. 1.

Nelsonville, Texas.

1907 - 1908.

Miss Lottie Meissner,
Teacher.

Supt. of Co., - - E. H. Sternenberg.

TRUSTEES.

Dr. J. Krolik, - - Mr. William Schupak.

Theresa Balusek	Erna Andreas
Hilda Balusek	Ella Schiller
Vlasta Schiller	Henry Rippel
Rose Schiller	Charles Stalmach
Alvina Motle	Eddie Stalmach
Annie Kamas	Adolph Andreas
Carrie Balusek	Charles Motle
Louise Schiller	William Kamas
Leonie Stalmach	Tom Kamas
Mathilda Schiller	Willie Motle
Emily Schillei	Micager Shelburne
Alvina Janovsky	Bennie Shelburne
Millie Pavelek	Charles Schiller
Tony Janovsky	Frank Schiller
Frances Janovsky	Frank Janovsky
Lena Andrews	F. Schiller
Tillie Bravenec	Louis Jochec
Lydia Stalmach	Edmund Stalmach
Vlasta Schiller	Edwin Stalmach

Nelsonville School

Novermber 30, 1911

NELSONVILLE SCHOOL Teacher: Ollie Burns

Oak Hill School

OAK HILL SCHOOL — 1915 -- front row, left to right, Edwin Krause, John Sebesta, Fritz Brast, Walter Surovik, Frank Jasek, Millie (Machinsky) Luedke, Lydie (Maresh) Pracek, Edna (Klump) Mikeska, Gertrude (Chernosky) Ray, Emilie (Placek) Masar, Milada (Maresh) Mikeska, Jessie (Huber) Frunka, Fannie (Mikeska) Janosky; second row, Alvin Bravenec, Jessie Frank, Leslie Doleshal, Willie Zajicek, August Hold, Mondrow Juergens, John Maresh, Sophie Elsik, Annie Surovik, Marie (Zajicek) Huff, Olga (Slacik) Schovajsa, Lillie (Charnak) Dipple, Annie (Bravenec) Chumchal, Esther (Kamas) Mikeska, Bertha (Machinsky) Ashorn; third row, Jerry Mikeska, Owen Schrader, Louis Janosky, Willie Maresh, Joe Kamas, Eldon Frank, Alvin Brast, Jerry Bravenec, Erna Bell (Juergens) Luhn, Marie (Huber) Koester, Tillie (Bravenec) Andreas, Angela (Zajicek) Richle, Mary Schroeder, Meta Schroeder, Emilie (Chernosky) Mooney, Lillie (Janosky) Engelholm; fourth row, John Surovik, John Zajicek, Edwin Hold, Joe Moudry, Gus Hartmann, Joe Janosky, teacher Hermina (Uhrik) Ripple, Lillie (Bravenec) Hold, Isabel (Huber) Frunka, Toni (Zajicek) Ueckert, Annie (Mikeska) Chernosky, Manilla (Chernosky) Pfeffer and Theresa (Placek) Macat.

Santa Anna School

Henry Ripple, Teacher

Santa Anna School

SANTA ANNA SCHOOL Teacher: John Ripple

Nelsonville School

NELSONVILLE SCHOOL Teacher: Rev. Anton Motycka

Jan and Anna Marek Bravenec
with daughters Alvina and Anna
1900

Dr. John and Emilie Lesikar Kroulik

HERMAN KRAUSE AND ANNIE BRAVENEC

(PHOTO CA. 1905)

Dr. John Kroulik Home in Nelsonville
Built in 1914, burned in 1948

WINCENT SAMUEL SHILLER FAMILY

(PHOTO CA. 1906)

BACK ROW: JOHN, CHARLES, LYDIA, ANNA, FRANCES, VINCENT, FRANK

FRONT ROW: EMILY, ROSE, ELLA, WINCENT S., EDWARD,
FRANCES (NEE KAMINECKY), LILLIE, VLASTA, MATHILDE

FRANCES AND ANNIE SHILLER

(PHOTO CA. 1895)

Stalmach Family - 1915

Back: John, Edwin, Leona, Charlie, Lydia, Edmond, Adolph
Front: Theresa, Eddie, John

Stalmach homeplace, New Bremen
John and Edwin Stalmach

"New" home near Nelsonville

Herman Krause Family - ca. 1915

Center: Terezie Shiller Krause and Herman Krause
Top Row, 2nd and 3rd from Left: Anna Bravenec Krause and Herman Krause

JAN JANECEK FAMILY - 1902 PHOTO

BACK ROW - EDWIN, LILLY, ANNA, ADELE, ANNA SHAW

FRONT ROW - JOHN, MARY (SECOND WIFE), JAN, PAULA SHAW

Edwin Janecek and Charles Shiller
Nelsonville, 1912

Maresh family photo ca. 1895

Taken on their homestead between Scranton Grove and Nelsonville.

Seated: Jan and Anna Haisler Mares (immigrated 1867)
Standing left to right are children Rosalie, Albina, William and Joseph

Hermina Uhrik

Victoria School February 8, 1928

Adolpf Benjamin Stepan Top row, 8th from left
Vlasta Frances Stepan Third row from bottom, 3rd from left

Theresie Slovak
at home near Nelsonville

Martin and Rosina Zapalac Stepan

"Grandma" Sefcik (at ca. age 75)
with granddaughters (L-R): Ester Sefcik and Lexie Minton

Jochek Children

1911

Franklin, Alice, Gilbert, Jessie, Alois

John Chernosky
Oak Hill - ca. 1915

Gardenia Matejka
Nelsonville

Joe Skalak
harvesting cotton

Frank and Frances Kroulik Langer
daughters (L-R): Libuna and Minnie
Frank's mother and 2nd husband Mr. Fisarek

Esterak Family

Seated: Sisters Ethel (Janovsky) and Lillie (Smith)
Standing: Unmarried Aunts Vinca and Rosalie, Uncle John

Ben and Charles Motl

Otto Andreas

Balusek Sisters

Mr. Hartman with Annie, Carrie, Mary, Rose, Hilda and Theresa

Olga Kroulik and Charles Stalmach

John Slacik and John Mikeska
at Oak Hill

Frank Pavelka and Ed Uhrik

Jochek Children

1911

Franklin, Alice, Gilbert, Jessie, Alois

Shiller Sisters

L-R: Rosie, Elsie, Louise, Bessie

Julia Supak
in her Parlor - 1908

Made in the USA
Coppell, TX
10 February 2024

28865790R10107